TEXT BY **WYNTON MARSALIS**

PHOTOGRAPHS BY **FRANK STEWART**

SWEET
SWING
BLUES

ON THE ROAD

W. W. NORTON & COMPANY ••• NEW YORK • LONDON

Text copyright © 1994 by Wynton Marsalis, photographs copyright © 1994 by Frank Stewart

First Edition

The text of this book is composed in **BODONI BOOK AND EUROSTILE BOLD EXTENDED**
with the display set in **EUROSTILE BOLD EXTENDED**
Composition by **COMCOM, INC. ALLENTOWN, PA.**
Manufacturing by **ARNOLDO MONDADORI EDITORE, VERONA, ITALY**
Book design by **BETH TONDREAU DESIGN**

LIBRARY OF CONGRESS CATALOGING-IN-PUBLICATION DATA
Marsalis, Wynton, 1961–
    Sweet swing blues on the road/Wynton Marsalis and Frank Stewart.
    p.   cm.
    1. Marsalis, Wynton, 1961-   .   2. Jazz musicians—United States—
    Biography.   I. Stewart, Frank.   II. Title.
    ML419.M3A3   1994
    788.9´2165´092—dc20
    [B]   93-4740

ISBN 0-393-03514-X

Printed in Italy

W. W. Norton & Company, Inc., 500 Fifth Avenue, New York, N.Y. 10110
W. W. Norton & Company Ltd., 10 Coptic Street, London WC1A 1PU

1 2 3 4 5 6 7 8 9 0

To the great Art Blakey, Bu.

WM

To the women in my life who made a difference:

Dorothy, Ruby, Mudear, Cora, Bea, Pam, Shelly, Jackie, Janet, Juanita, Cliffton, Mary,

Peggy, Paula, Jeanne, Ntozaké, Tei-sing, Sing, Bining, and last but certainly not least,

my beautiful wife, Halima, who sacrificed and understood.

FS

CONTENTS

1. CALL

The first thing that young trumpeters realize is: we can play loud. Louder than anybody else in the band except the drummer.

WE GROW UP hearing that trumpeters blew down the walls of Jericho, that Gabriel's trumpet announces the will of God, and that the largest and hippest of all animals, the elephant, has a trunk mostly (we think) for trumpeting. These grandiose images shape the classic trumpet persona: brash, impetuous, cocky, cool, in command. Anyone who has ever played in a band knows that if the conductor stops rehearsal because a fight breaks out, if somebody takes your girlfriend, if a tasteless practical joke is pulled, if someone challenges every executive decision no matter how trivial, it's got to be a trumpet player. That's just how we are.

The instrument itself, an elaborate megaphone attached to lips, gives trumpeters the confidence to play loud, louder, and then loudest. But if we play long enough, the softer side of the instrument will beckon, almost imperceptibly, sweetly goading us to find a drop of humility underneath that mountain of trumpetian ego. One drop, and then, even against your will, you discover that music can and will flow through the bell of your instrument. ALL YOU HAVE TO DO IS PRACTICE. (That's all.) Then all of that braying, honking, and spraying becomes playing. Yes, and playing is always welcomed, because it involves elegance and style, sophistication and the control of power. Good manners.

By merely trying to play, you reach back, even if unknowingly, into

the lineage of trumpeters throughout history and become one of Gabriel's children. You can close your eyes and pretend to be an ancient herald, blowing a leg bone or an elephant tusk, or one of those horns that the old, cold Vikings sounded from their raiding boats to strike fear and awe in the hearts of those about to be plundered. Hold the trumpet up proudly, and you can become a priest, a shaman, or a griot. You call the community to assembly, call the children home.

That's what they say the great New Orleans trumpet legend Buddy Bolden liked to do with his horn, and I guess that's what we all like to do. Impart important information with horn in hand.

But don't get the wrong impression. The trumpet is also cheeky and spoiled. You have to make it respect you. It's like breaking in a proud

horse. Convince it that you are the boss, and your purpose will be served. When thrown—and you will be thrown—jump immediately back on with deliberation and style. The trumpet trumpets. A trombone doesn't trombone, a violin doesn't violin. You control the wind, push air through the horn like a lightning bolt from the hand of Zeus. Elemental power harnessed and directed from deep inside. The sound crackles out into the air. It excites and then leaves a hot glow. Then you have to rest, and listen.

Not to say that listening is necessarily a restful activity. There are many ways to listen, and as for musicians, if we don't listen, we can't play. In the band we always say: Learn to have fun checking the other cats out. That's one of the great lessons in jazz music: make room for someone else, help them sound good, then use a part of what they are playing to sound good yourself. Whenever somebody plays something good on our bandstand, we jokingly cup our hands together, reach down, scoop up the sound, and pour it all over our faces like we're bathing in it.

The warmth of a beautiful sound massages your soul. Like when you've been inside all day: in the late afternoon you go outside and the sun hits your face, but in that instant it becomes a caress. Intense, but not too hot or too bright, it warms your whole body up just right. Or the first time you kiss the woman you've been wanting to kiss for a long time. Have mercy! Just the sweetness and warmth of it makes you want to holler or scream. But you don't, you bask in it, it just feels good.

Trumpeting is as old as dust, but it wasn't until Haydn wrote his concerto in 1796 that the trumpet began to come into its own. Before this concerto, the trumpet was mainly used for fanfares and an occasional punctuation or two. Every now and then the high-pitched, oboe-sounding baroque trumpets would get a choice melody. But the lower, trumpet-sounding trumpets were relegated to playing with the timpani or field drums. The addition of keys gave the trumpet extra notes in the lower and middle registers, and that's where most of the whispering and crooning takes place. Not to say that the keyed trumpet on which the Haydn was first performed sounded particularly majestic (folks said it sounded more like a wounded duck). With the advent of valves in 1814, the trumpet became more and more capable in greater areas of expression (as well as not duck-sounding).

But it wasn't until the twentieth century that the trumpet became deep down funny, seriously sensual, unaffectedly noble, and, truth be told, downright profane. This took place in New Orleans, Louisiana, issued from the

horns of jazzman Buddy Bolden and his progeny, the greatest of which was Louis Armstrong. Buddy Bolden, then Bunk Johnson, Freddie Keppard, then King Oliver, and then Louis. That's the roll call. They made the trumpet sound like many instruments at once. They played with a real intense vibrato, herald style.

Buddy Bolden could play so loud, he could make the rain stay up in the sky. Then he could turn around and play a song so sweet, it would make your mama cry. Bunk Johnson had a tone so dark and smoky, he could play the blues at high noon and bring the nighttime on. King Oliver could make the trumpet sound like a chicken, cat, dog, elephant, lion, or a woman sighin'. Freddie Keppard could make a horn laugh till the blues were long

gone. And Louis Armstrong did whatever he wanted to do whenever he wanted to do it, be it testifying, cosigning, or signifyin'. Yes, these were men who shouted and whispered with style and accuracy.

Whispering makes listening intimate. When you can sustain a whisper, you are reintroduced to your best self. Yes, indeed. Intensity without volume. And sustained intensity equals ecstasy. I notice when older musicians play the blues, they always play the end of a phrase a lot softer than the beginning. This makes you listen through the whole phrase. They catch your attention and then make you listen.

That's playing blues. The blues provides a whole world of cries, shouts, and smears to play with, as well as a direct route to adult expression. The blues has psychological

complexity. You have to strain to propel some blues out of a horn because the blues reconciles opposites. You put something beautiful right on top of something ugly. Take something from the whorehouse and put it right next to something from the church. That's the blues—just like life. It has a Venus's-flytrap quality; you think it's one thing until you get inside, then you realize it's another thing entirely. That's how an E is. This note can be hit with more valve combinations—first and second, third, no valves down, or all three down—than any other. It will sing, cry, laugh, and croon for you.

When I was growing up, we used to play the dozens. See who could come up with the best put-downs of another. Many a fight started over some too-accurate observation in the heat of a verbal exchange. We also used to refer to the dozens as calling someone out. Calling as in the clarion sound of the trumpet. And just as accuracy, directness, and quickness are required of a dozens champion, so, too, of an improvisor of jazz music. But instead of issuing put-downs, the jazz musician passes out tones that make you feel good.

This requires courage. A put-down is its own defense, you know what the response will be. Whereas kindness allows for an unpredictable range of responses. Ugliness requires less involvement, so it always finds new recruits.

But playing something of beauty in public, or privately, requires a direct honesty, a simplicity. And a direct emotion is almost always returned, even from a large audience, whose feeling may be cold or warm, bored or excited, or ambivalent. Your intent to deliver this thing of beauty has to be pure enough to overcome fear of what the response may be. Then you might get the response you want.

Anyway, even the most intimate details of what you have to say through your horn, the audience already knows. Because they live it. Our job as musicians is to play as much of life as we can understand. If we don't listen, not just to what is said but to what is felt, we can't play. Buddy

Bolden liked to listen. And his reply, issued through the red-hot bell of a
blues trumpet in the streets, parks, and dance halls of the Crescent City,
New Orleans, Louisiana, still resounds.

> I thought I heard Buddy Bolden say,
> "Shake it, break it, take it away."

> I thought I heard Buddy Bolden call,
> "This is how they do it down in Funky Butt Hall."

> I thought I heard Buddy Bolden shout,
> "I gon' blow this quail till my tongue hang out."

2. RESPONSE

"You can't make it alone. You have to have loyalty and commitment from others to play this music."

THE LEADER OF A JAZZ band has to exert the control of no control. Each musician in the band has to feel free to be creative and reach for unusual corners in their personalities. I try to provide a context for every man to develop his potential and feel as relaxed and expressive as possible. The musical directions we pursue come directly out of the collective experiences of the band. The hardest part of leading is understanding how to make the expression of differing viewpoints sound harmonious. And, in this part of the twentieth century, developing a philosophy that will teach the musicians the meanings of jazz music.

Sometimes you have personality clashes. These are inevitable, because people who possess high levels of creativity don't like being told what to do. Men and women who want to play jazz, especially in these times, must have a lot of pride and stamina. They are individuals, and that's what I like to hear. I love the sound of the ultimate extension of someone's abilities. The willful desire to play something great. Play it with feeling, power, and confidence.

You can't make a band feel obligated to your conception, even if they're well paid. On the bandstand, maintaining seriousness and a desire to swing and sound good—every time—is the only thing that makes good musicians want to play with you. When everyone chooses to participate, that's when the music is beautiful. When playing, the jazz musician can't let anything get in the way of that choice.

One time or another, everybody in the band says, "Man, I'm dealing with so much in my personal life, coming out here is like escaping." On the bandstand we're in an idyllic world. We're all concentrating and trying to work out our problems collectively by expressing ourselves in music. This music is like therapy. The blues itself is a healing agent, a Greek comedy and tragedy rolled into one. It's mythology in the hands of a jazz band, like the fables of old Ethiope, who they called Aesop.

The bandstand is an arena of equality ruled only by ability. You have to play something to establish who you are. I may be the official leader of the band, but I better play some music, or the music will run right over me. Whoever is playing the most music at any given moment is the leader. Cold but true, musically speaking.

When you're on the road as much as we are, the band becomes like a second family. That's what Herlin always says. Being in such close quarters for extended periods of time leads to different frictions, but we always try to work things out through open discussion. It's also important to know when to leave people alone. Art Blakey said, "There's nothing wrong with letting cats call you a motherfucker sometimes and get shit off of their minds." They're grown men, and sometimes that's a part of it. A leader shouldn't try to control every decision on the bandstand. Get musicians you respect and then trust their vision, even when it is different from your

own. The only necessary ingredients are faith and loyalty to the basic conception of the band.

"You can't make it alone. You have to have loyalty and commitment from others to play this music." Those are the words of the J Master, Marcus Roberts, one of the finest musicians in the world. The J Master is chairman of the board of directors of the band, our pianist emeritus. He's funny, soulful, and intelligent. The cats love him. He and I have a deep spiritual connection.

The J Master renewed my faith in jazz music. In 1984 half of my first band left to play rock music. I thought maybe no one with that real fire and talent in our generation wanted to play jazz—not enough external rewards for swinging. Then I called the J Master as a last resort. We had been having phone conversations off and on since 1980, and I had heard him play several times. I didn't really dig his playing that much, but when he talked—have mercy! He would say things I had never heard from our generation. Serious ideas about music and culture, adulthood, racism. Well thought out and carefully considered, not just a regurgitation of popular clichés. Plus he wanted to swing—bad.

I was worried about dealing with him on the road, because I had never dealt with anyone who was blind. Well, when Marcus came to my apartment in Brooklyn to practice in 1985, my understanding of what it takes to play this music changed. He was not bullshitting! First he knew all of our recorded music. Then he would get up early in the morning and practice until late at night. He was like a sponge, he soaked up all kinds of information: musical, intellectual, spiritual. He brought another level of seriousness to what remained of the band and, strangely, another level of intimacy. Just little things like making sure J's tie was straight or him holding your arm when we went places, it made us all more aware of the importance of looking out for one another.

J can eat three big-ass dinners and not gain a pound. And loves him some Coca-Cola. He sometimes speaks in the J Voice, a cross between John Huston and Ronald Reagan. It belongs to the bank manager who says, "Well, Mr. Marsalis, there's no loans (for Negroes) today. We understand you're starting a new business venture, and, uh, we wish you well. God bless you." Or the kindly contemporary overseer: "I like my Negroes natural, real, with plenty of feeling and uh, ignorant. Just be quiet, do your work, and leave the deciding to me."

For a long time I thought, "Man, this cat is strange." One day I got up the courage to ask, "Say, man, are you all right, man, is something wrong with you?" He said, "Man, that's just this voice I talk in when people are bullshitting."

The J Master loves football and Monopoly. If you want to lose some money, bet with him. In or on anything. He invents strange games, too. Like the game show called *That's Your Ass*. If you lose, they give you two hot irons and put you into a cage with a hungry lion. J is deeply perceptive, and all of the cats love talking to him. He can give you expert romantic counsel and break down all kinds of ways to address other problems of life. I never make a serious decision without consulting the J Master.

When J left the band in 1991, I cried like a baby. But he still sits in with us now and then, and still learns all of our music, even those long two-hour pieces. When he plays, the entire history of the jazz piano resonates. Styles that were practically dead are resuscitated, and a style that has never existed is created. He is a true original, a real jazzman, not afraid to swing and play the blues with authority, intelligence, abandon, and soul. Yes, with soul. We had a saying about the J Master. It goes with the melody of the first song he recorded with the band, "J Mood." "He's in no mood to be fucked with, he's no mood for bullshit, J Mood, J Mood, J Mood, J Mood J—Mood J Mood J Mood J Mood." But if you followed him around with a movie camera, the result would definitely be a comedy.

WYCLIFFE GORDON loves to play some country, tailgate trambone. He is from Augusta, Georgia, and joined the band in 1989. He hadn't played that much jazz. At the time he was playing electric bass with a funk band in Tallahassee, working in a Pizza Hut, and attending school at Florida A & M. But he inherited the spirit of this music at age thirteen after listening to Louis Armstrong's "Keyhole Blues," and to this day he loves him some Louis Armstrong. He stood on our bandstand for one year just listening and trying to understand how to play this music.

Wycliffe can hear music naturally. Harmonies and melodies reveal themselves to him quickly. He memorizes music rapidly and is also a very good composer and arranger.

He has a tremendous range of personality—introspective, funny, he has a spiritual side, he reads his Bible. But he will put his foot in someone's boodie if he is disrespected. And that is a large foot. He is the strongest member of the band, can throw a football about seventy yards. For real! On the bus at night he and Veal put weightlifting belts on over their pajamas, and then they sit down and eat a big-ass meal. Veal fix him a quadruple-decker peanut butter and jelly sandwich, and Wycliffe eat him a whole pile of food—potato chips, pickles, luncheon meat sandwiches. Then they drink a Diet Coke and go to bed. They sleep on all that food with the belt on. Yep, and the belt hooks it all up. I see those belts all the time, but I never see them lifting any weights.

Wycliffe's nickname is Pine Cone because he is country by choice. He's the kind of person can fix broken doors with gum wrappers and such.

Pine Cone can fix his own instrument and cut his own hair. He can play any instrument in the band—with style. Trumpet, bass, piano, drums, even the clarinet. He is the perfect musician in a group context, because he plays things that fit. A great jazz musician because he is spontaneous and not afraid to be his best self in public.

Cone is a good teacher, too. When young trombonists come backstage, he's very patient with them. He tried to teach me how to swim, but I nearly drowned him learnin'.

He sometimes wears his tie so you can see both sides of it. The little side you normally wear in the back, he wears in front. He paid for the whole tie, so he wants you to see the whole tie. That's how he plays the trombone—all of it, all the time.

THE BASS is the band's heartbeat. You need a blue-collar worker, dependable, steady, and relentless, to play it. Reginald Veal is such a man. He understands the poetic qualities of his instrument, knows how to make the bass voice resonate in different situations, has a great pulse, loves to

groove, and plays with intelligence. He is diligent about mastering his instrument and calls bassists in the various cities we play for lessons and insights. He has to be well dressed and smelling right. Veal's bathroom shelf holds enough talcs and perfumes for the ground floor of a department store. His suitcase is the heaviest in the band. He presses his drawers.

Many young bassists hit random and illogical notes when constructing bass lines. Not Veal. His lines are well heard, logical, and melodic, like his attire. He also plays the trombone, piano, and drums. We call him Swing Doom. Swing is for the feeling, Doom is for the sound.

Veal grew up playing church music with his father, who sings, and he has that church feeling. Sometimes his daddy comes on the road to check us out, and we see where Veal gets all of that soul.

Veal loves the wood sound of the bass—Doom, Doom, Doom; he's the first bassist of our generation to play without the amp. This teaches us all to play softer and listen, to swing.

My father would always tell me about Reginald Veal. He would say, "Boy, you got to check out Veal. He has it all. The feel, the pride, and the intelligence." Veal is from New Orleans, so whenever I came into town, he would be on the set to play and talk about what was going on in New York. He and Noel Kendrick, a young drummer, had a regular weekend gig with my father at Tyler's Beer Gardens, a local club where you could get a dozen oysters for a dollar. After the gig we would go to Noel's house and jam from 2:00 to 5:30 in the morning, and then we would talk out on the corner for another two or three hours, and then we would get breakfast at Bailey's. Sometimes we wouldn't jam, we would just stand out among the late night goings-on, focused on conversation about the swing.

You got to watch Veal. Once he came to my house to rehearse and some people he had previous problems with were present. Veal pulled his bass out of the case. Then he pulled his gun out, put it on the table, and said to me, "You ready to shed, bruh?" Those present remembered they had other, less important things to do and left early.

But Veal is also the ballad king of the band. He loves Nat King Cole, Billie Holiday, Johnny Hartman, and he keeps something sweet on in his room.

Veal got married on the sly. Just showed up one day with a wedding ring on, married to Kim. They met at Wes's wedding; Desi, Wes's wife, introduced them.

The bass and the drums are the heart and soul of a band. Like the offensive and defensive lines of a football team, they are the team. If you have a sorry line, you'll never win. With Swing Doom on the line you always have a chance to win, because he never gives up. He's not that type of man.

TODD WILLIAMS is the Deacon. As in that strong, devout deacon who can be depended upon to praise with intensity and accuracy. I met him in St. Louis when he was sixteen years old. He came backstage and looked serious. So I asked Branford to let Todd play his tenor saxophone. He sounded okay, but more than that he was hungry to learn. Delfeayo sent him some tapes of the greatest saxophonist in history. Two years later he came to my hotel room when we passed through St. Louis and played Coltrane's entire solo on "Crescent" from memory. He has the discipline required for mastery.

The saxophone is a thinking man's instrument. It has all those keys and can be played continuously much longer than brass instruments. That reed is more forgiving than cold brass. This gives saxophonists more time to think. Coleman Hawkins, the father of the jazz tenor saxophone, was called Bean because he used his head when playing. And the whole lineage of the saxophone is full of thinkers who created intricate styles: Lockjaw Davis, Don Byas, Frankie Trumbauer, Charlie Parker, Sonny Rollins, Coltrane, Joe Henderson, Wayne Shorter, and so on. The Deacon is in that mold. Whenever I write something very difficult to play, stuff in odd meters or with abstract harmonic relationships, give it to the Deacon. He will figure it out and play it.

Saxophonists seem to get along with each other. They don't have the cocky disposition of trumpeters. Except for Sidney Bechet, but then he was also a trumpeter. I think it has something to do with reeds. They are always shaving, licking, looking at, or adjusting their reeds. And they're still not satisfied. This conditions them to working things out.

The Deacon knows how to play in a section and will phrase music in the exact style of whomever he is playing with. We brought him on and off the road from 1986 until 1988, when he joined the band. On, to feel the swing. Off, to practice some more. He has added the clarinet and soprano sax to the list of instruments he plays and can be counted upon to practice even during rigorous travel periods. I always make sure not to get a room next to his.

Deacon can imitate voices, is very funny, but generally keeps to himself. I was shocked when he called me in the summer of 1987 to come on the road. He was working on a furniture truck and that strengthened his resolve to play this music.

The Deacon is a devout Christian. He left the band in 1991 to see if he wanted to do something else. (He also hates the travelling.) He came back in 1992, then left again and finally in 1993. He wants to play only church music. We miss his musicianship, but we know that whatever church he plays in will be swinging—hard. One other thing: never ask the Deacon to critique a meal; he even likes airplane food.

I KNOW we've been off too long when Wes Anderson calls me and starts talking about getting back out on the road. Wes always says the same thing, "I'm ready for some more of that glorious swing." He's always swinging day or night. If he's not playing, he's got his headphones on, listening to Sonny Stitt, Gene Ammons, Hank Mobley: bebop, blues, and hardcore swing. He was raised that way. His father is a jazz drummer. If you saw him watching Wes at our concerts, you would know what being proud is. He should be. Wes plays the alto saxophone with glistening soul.

Wes and Veal attended Southern University in Baton Rouge, Louisiana, together. Swinging on the yard with Bat, as in Alvin Batiste, instructor of jazz at Southern and one of the world's great men of music. Wes moved to Baton Rouge after he got married to Desi in 1990. Seduced by the South. Desi comes out on the road sometimes to listen and support Wes. She'll also tell him, "You've got to play some more horn, baby." He loves to play for her.

Wes first came to play with the band in Cincinnati in 1985, and got sent back to school. He practiced hard and came back out here in 1988, for good. People love to be around Wes, he's accepting of everyone and nonjudgmental. They can feel the love. He's the type of cat the older musicians call a sweetheart. His personality comes through his playing. He has a warm, sweet, lyrical sound, that's why we call him Warm Daddy. He likes his grits and gravy. He likes his chicory coffee. He likes to smoke his cigarettes and wear those little soulful hats. He wakes up on a good vibe. The only things he don't like are bugs, late food—and people going into

double time when he's soloing; then he steps off the mike and makes it clear an adjustment is necessary.

We have musical conversations on the phone. I'll call him and play some blues. His horn, which is always out, will respond. Then we go back and forth, and whoever plays the most soulful shit will bust out laughing. If he really cuts my head, he'll just say, "Well," and hang up.

Wes is number one in the band at being on time. But he still loves to hang out. Late. He and I always go to the jam sessions after the gigs, and we tease each other about who's gonna cut whose head. Once, in Brussels, we played a tune called "Invitation" and he gave me a merciless trim. I got off the bandstand and tried to sit down to escape further damage, but Wes followed me around the club with what seemed like a rush of fire pouring out of the bell. "No, thank you, I'll take a cognac and some water. Please." For two months he ribbed me: "Brussels." Wes can play plenty of piano, too. Plenty.

He hates to sound bad. When he's not playing good, leave Wes alone. Fortunately, that only happens once or twice a year. And no one is ever there but him.

BILLY HIGGINS says that a drummer has to be kind. We call Herlin Riley Homey, because he is from New Orleans and makes everyone feel at home. He possesses the essence of soul. This means that when he is on the scene, people are having a good time. If he's eating, he'll always ask, "You want some, bruh?" If we're playing basketball, he'll make sure everyone gets in the game, he doesn't mind passing the ball. On the bandstand he swings and grooves.

Herlin has a real spiritual connection to the drums. He started out as a trumpeter, but switched in his teens to drums. Trumpet and drums have been connected throughout history, in worship and war. Herlin is a member of a New Orleans musical family, the Lasties, and grew up listening to his grandfather tap out various deeply rooted and soulful Crescent City grooves on tables, with spoons, or on body. Drumming is in his genes. If he was in a community of drummers, the elders would pick him out at the age of three or four to study with the master drummer.

Herlin is comfortable with his gift and he doesn't mind practicing, so he continues to learn new things about playing at an age when many musicians are set in their ways. He's not old in years, he's just thirty-six. But the style of most musicians is set by their thirties; and if they've received recognition by that time, forget it. Herlin keeps growing.

Homey is from the 9th Ward of New Orleans. "Lower 9 don't mind dyin'." Just think about how that sounds to know what it means. He grew up playing in church, so he knows that tradition. He can play the tambourine, the washboard, anything you can hit, he can play.

From Johnny Dodds to Jo Jones to Kenny Clarke to Max Roach, Philly Joe Jones, Art Blakey, and Elvin Jones, a drummer's style determines the sound of the band. With the exception of Baby Dodds, I have known all of these men, and they have a combination of down-home hipness and willful sophistication. A sense of earned aristocracy that is the result of years of study and the highest level of performance on the only instrument created by jazz music. They almost never rest during a performance and provide intensity as well as organize the dynamics of events in the form of a song.

The drum set is actually many instruments. The sounds of the animal skins, the wood, and the metal combine all the elements. And what about the brushes! A sensual sound like a soft breeze, or so many tongues slowly stroking salty epidermis.

Homey is a great dancer, a prerequisite for a drummer, and a very fine athlete. He loves some New Orleans food, red beans and rice, gumbo filé, and his sugar with some chicory coffee in it. He has five children, he knows responsibility. He can play some pool, too! If you don't watch him, he will hustle you at the table. He has the singular distinction of being voted the least timely band member, a badge he wears with honor and strives hard to maintain. He is the king of the one-liners, like "A chicken ain't nothing but a bird" and "Everything shining ain't gold" (but his drumming sure is).

I FIRST HEARD Eric Reed when he was fourteen years old at the Community School in Los Angeles. The dean of the school, Joe Thayer, was also the dean of the Eastern Music Festival, which is a summer classical music camp I attended when I was in high school. He called me and said, "Man, I

have a student here who really can play some jazz piano. Can you give me your father's number, so I can make sure he gets the proper instruction?" My father referred him to Harold Battiste, a great New Orleans musician who was living in Los Angeles at the time. Harold taught Eric the New Orleans way, relaxed and with feeling.

Whenever we came through Los Angeles, Eric Reed would be there. When Marcus Roberts first joined the band, many musicians questioned the wisdom of hiring him. After hearing Marcus for the first time, fifteen-year-old Eric called me and said, "Who is Marcus, and where did you find him? He is unbelievable." That's when I knew Eric would be a great musician. A lot of what determines the rate and nature of a young jazz musician's development is their ability to figure out who is actually playing something worthwhile. With the celebration of worthlessness in our culture, very few youngsters have the opportunity or desire to develop their taste, or accept the fact that there is such a thing as refining sensibilities.

That is why I am particularly proud of Eric Reed's development. He possesses the highest levels of pure musical abilities. But that's no assurance of first-class musicianship. Real musicianship can only be developed when put to the test of discipline and hard work. And it never stops. Eric joined the band in 1990 and was sent home, with love, in 1991. He got a piano teacher, continued to come support the music, and came back out here in 1992 with a greater sense of urgency. He is dedicated and understands what the modern jazz piano requires. His belief in this music is projected in his sound.

Eric grew up playing in the church (his father was a gospel singer and is now a minister). You can hear the signifying in his playing—all of the time. He travels with about two hundred CDs of various styles: classical, gospel, all types of jazz. And loves him some Art Blakey. He and Wes are the tune doctors in the band. Between the two of them they know some two thousand songs. Eric is peaceful by nature, but you better not even think of taking food off his plate. When food is involved, no prisoners.

HERB HARRIS played tenor and soprano sax during Todd's first sabbatical. I first heard him play at a high school in Washington, D.C. Later he attended Florida A & M with Wycliffe. They both worked in a Pizza Hut and played an occasional gig or two. When we recorded a Christmas album, he played the baritone sax and clarinet for us. I didn't really know the range of the baritone sax, so I was writing notes all off the horn for him. He was playing 'em, too. He didn't know where the note was either, he'd just honk, "Is that it?" "Yeah, that's it, play that." A low C or something a half step lower than the horn is supposed to go.

One night at Blues Alley in D.C., Herb played the most moving solo I have ever heard on a slow minor blues. He just held one note on the clarinet for a whole chorus. But that note had so much feeling, almost desperation in it, that the audience applauded wildly. "What was happening with that?" I asked him. "Man, I was unfamiliar with that key and afraid to hit another note," was the reply. We call Herb Triple H. Hibernatin' Herb Harris. He will sleep fifteen hours on the bus and then go to his room for a nap.

BEN WOLFE is from Portland, Oregon. He likes to wear his ties with a little knot. He is one of the few musicians to play with us without a rehearsal. He took Veal's place for about one month when Veal had dental surgery. Wolfé, as we call him, is deadly serious about swinging and sounding good. He has a large sound and fine powers of concentration. He has many interests and is fun to talk to as well as very humorous. He is an excellent mimic and always comes to work ready to play.

CHARNETTE MOFFET, the Netman, used to come to my apartment almost every day in the early 1980s when he was fourteen, fifteen years old. He'd be visiting Little John Longo, who was living with me and Branford while attending high school at Music and Art in New York City. We lived on Bleecker Street in Manhattan, and Big John, Little John's father and my original trumpet teacher in New Orleans, was living on Long Island. So for matters of convenience Little John stayed with us. Charnette also attended Music and Art. He had all kinds of energy and loved to play, clown around, and recite his favorite rap song, "Give It to the Netman."

They were always talking about Charnette's ability to play the bass. I thought it was just a joke. One day we all went into a pawnshop, and there was an old beat-up bass in the corner. "Why don't you play that bass?" I asked him. "Boom, Boom, Boom," he started pulling all kinds of sound and groove out of that bass. I was stunned. This was a fourteen-year-old boy sounding like a real bass player in the early 1980s, when you never heard a dark, full bass sound from young musicians. He is not afraid to get callouses on his fingers. He was born to swing on the acoustic bass. He can't help it.

FARID BARON took over the piano chair for a while. He has a rhythmic, humorous sound that is totally unpredictable. We call him Skoodlieoop, 'cause he'd try to play phrases beyond his technical command on the instrument and that's how it would sound. We also call him Freeze, 'cause he's so cool. Freeze is just as cool as he wants to be. In 1988 he was part of an all-star high school band of students from New York, Philadelphia, and D.C. that I conducted. When I introduced him at the first concert, all the girls started hollering. He had his vest on, with his hair all pressed and cute. Freeze is an original. He sits on the bus at night, do-rag on head, pontificating on the merits of the Philly cheese steak. With us coming from New Orleans, land of the po-boy sandwich, he can't get too much respect. He is also a brilliant student, had a full scholarship to Drexel in science, but was attracted to the swing. He is the house pianist at Ordlieb's Jazz Haus in Philadelphia in the truest sense of the word because he lives right above the club. And is still late to work. After he got married to his sweetheart, Charisse, he became even cooler. Now we call him Deep Freeze, and when we really want to be accurate we say, "Where there is Freeze, there is peace."

OUR SOUND MAN is David Robinson. Sound man is his job description, but in reality he's the eighth member of the band. After a concert in Bern, Switzerland, a musician from another band said, "Man, you all sounded good. But what about that sound man? That's like having another cat in the band."

David Robinson has many nicknames. Sugar Rob, because he has mastered the language of courtship. But also Toon Yab Scob, Sugar Hob, Hoon, and Hin Yab.

Sugar Hob is greatly interested in the world. Wherever we go, he takes a tour of the city, interacts with people, and makes sure to participate in the life of the place—whatever that is.

Rob is one of the world's great hangers. He will hang till all hours and return to the hotel as the sun rises, appetite for life fully satisfied—for the moment.

Toon Yab Scob loves to swing and listen to jazz music. Many nights he sweats as hard at the sound board as the band does on stage, helping our sound overcome sorry acoustics.

Rob loves to eat him some soul food—collard greens, black-eyed peas, yams, smothered pork chops, cornbread, baby back ribs: smokestack lightning.

Hoon is from Houston, and he loves being a Texan. He wears his hat with dignity and pride. He loves to be clean. Attired in splendor, he is truly Sweet Sugar Rob, Toon Yab Scob, David Robinson.

3. CHORUS

Eight o'clock P.M. all over the world. Good-time time. Up steps, over wires into an arena of combat. Enemy is the blues on high ground, stubbornly refusing to be laid low by grown-ups engaged in (mere) child's play. Playing the blues. All over the world feet shuffle in the direction of battle—Doom, Doom, Baummm-Baummm, Dooom. "A" is struck to accompany the clattering of trap set and the clapping of hands that have waited for the arrival of musicians now adjusting slides and burning cork on metal. Tuning instruments to make tonight's engagement a more even match. The blues are not to be played with.

SOME HAVE COME TONIGHT to savor the sweet taste of victory, some to observe coldly, still others have already decided that the pitiless eyes of defeat will stare these musicians into an embarrassing silence. Whatever the perspectives, they assure victory by their presence. *They* have become, even if unwittingly, *us* in the process of turning the blues back, with style and accuracy.

We have no need for hysteria or the comfort of a mass-media brainwashing that would have us declare that the many men stamped out under the large blue feet of Goliath—blue with the blood of would-be heroes whose lives were extinguished so quickly the air had no time to turn it red—were the same as one young David, wise before his years and armed with the ability to swing an idea toward the heavens. Grown-ups engaged in (mere) child's play. We are assembled to take part in a display of skill and

a trial of tuneful arms. This could be any point on the long and distinguished time line of the human search for a lasting and profound happiness. But this is the end of the twentieth century. All of us will settle for two and one-half to three hours of jazz music. It is eight o'clock P.M. all over the world and the engagement has just begun.

Out on the hardwood slowly raising, to grasp a microphone, the hand that moments before had checked a zipper potentially left unzipped. "Good evening, ladies and gentlemen. Thank you for coming out this evening. We hope you enjoy yourselves. Because we are here to swing." I start every concert with these words, then introduce the band.

"Enjoy yourselves," thinks T Bone. "This is three weeks of my party money invested in these tickets. These boys better be swinging, and Adrienne better dig it—and me, too. I been trying for five years to get her out on a date. She sure is looking good, though. Damn."

Now I'm calling the first tune with a little story that I will say is the song's meaning. It's not true, but sounds good. People laugh. I've contemplated this tune all afternoon. We plunge into the silent concentration of group improvisation. A concentration that has taken years to develop.

"Are we in tune? Yes. In balance? No, I'm playing too loud. Relax. Solo. Listen to everyone. Develop themes. Why is Veal playing that damn D-natural? He's trying to throw me. No, he is being creative. Don't be afraid, just catch it the next time around. Interact with Herlin. Listen. Develop to climax. Relax and solo. Here comes Wes. Come on now, let's swing. Veal and Herlin are working tonight. Yes, that's it. Take the song out."

We are snatched from the silence of listening and reacting into the sound of applause. *"Did they like that song? Who hasn't soloed? What to play next?* Okay, a groove song for those who like the Spanish tinge. Thank you very much, and now . . ."

Adrienne says, "I like the way they look, just playing. It looks dignified, makes me feel proud." T Bone breathes a sigh of relief. "But that song was too fast." He puts his arm around her. "That's all right, baby, they gonna play something slow. They better."

Mrs. Martin, she's unimpressed. She remembers Duke Ellington's band. Rex Stewart was her favorite. She remembers when bebop came in, too. She never did like Dizzy or Parker. That song sounded too much like them.

Groovin' in the key of E. People on the bandstand forgetting cues and missing ensemble passages, but still the groove feels good. Red and hot. Me and Cone phrasing together with plunger mutes like two choirboys drawing something nasty on a back pew. *"Is Cone going to play short or long? What about the long note? How long? Yeah, okay, now half-speed. Yes. Now gradually slower. Good."*

Wycliffe plays perfectly, making small adjustments to the improvised phrasings with which I test his reflexes. As he shoots me a quick glance, we smile in recognition of what he has done, and . . .

"My solo," Wycliffe thinks. *"Slide the trombone. Listen to Eric. Play with the rhythm Veal has introduced. Converse with him for a minute. End gracefully. Don't blast on the horn. The hell with it. Yes. Blast one good one. Feel guilty."*

"Man, don't feel guilty," I tell him. "We both have to learn to control these brass instruments."

"Damn, bruh! It's hard."

"I know. I been struggling with it longer than you."

Eric has been soloing: *"I wish they would shut the fuck up while I'm playing. Hmm, okay, Veal. They were talking about the music, it's cool. E sure is a hard-ass key."*

We are taking the song out. Homey grooves through the vamp playing things we have never heard before. We all smile. Much of the time when playing we only hear melodies, rhythms, harmonies, and textures. But we also think these thoughts trying to make potential chaos coherent, moment to moment. That's a jazz band. Continuous musical adjustment to solve problems that have never existed.

Professor Fernandez has brought his high school band to tonight's concert. They comment on various technical aspects of what they have heard. Nathan is their best trumpeter, first chair all-state. He has all of Marsalis's recordings. The students look at him as particularly difficult passages are played. "What about that, Nathan? Can you do that?" Nathan says nothing, because he has stayed up many a night listening to these same men swinging on CDs. He has read every word of Crouch's liner notes and studied every picture as if it were part of a recurring dream. Now here they are and better than on the records. He has nothing to say. He will miss nothing tonight, especially by answering dumb questions from the uninitiated.

Now it's time to play a slow sweet one. Me and Eric. "This next tune is a Hoagy Carmichael composition entitled 'Stardust.'" As I lift the horn, out of the corner of my eye I spot Adrienne and T Bone. *"Damn! She is fine. He's kind of corny looking, but I hope this ballad helps him out. 'Sometimes I wonder why I spend the lonely nights . . .'"*

Slowing pushing myself out into an audience of strangers become coconspirators in an intrigue of intimacy. Telling of broken, mended, and rejuvenated hearts, a confluence of romantic experiences. Going beyond thought so as to play all of myself. Notes cascade off walls. *"Hope Eric hears this tempo. Where's the pulse? Yass! Let's stay on this vibe. Put your arm around her, T Bone."* Play pure melody, no runs. And so it goes. Attempting to spread generous helpings of a tone honed through years of attempting. Trying to play many ways at once, like making love to a woman you will never please. Horn raised at a forty-five-degree angle, pointed like a cannon to blow flowers to the many who have come to be serenaded.

"That's what we paid to hear," shouts someone as the final clarion note rings. "That's what we came here for." Once again make consonant the dissonance of that final tone. Nathan hangs his head. His fellow students think he is jealous or ashamed to have thought himself to be, on occasion, a great trumpeter. "What about that, Nathan? Huh?" His head hangs lower to hide the tears that cling to his eyes. Tears of joy at the recognition of someone unafraid to say it's alright to let people know you love them, the music, and the horn. He thinks of how hard he will practice upon returning home.

"Were you trying to put your hand on my breast?" Adrienne asks T Bone.

"Nah, baby, I was just moving with a note he played and my hand slipped. Say, I noticed you start rubbing my leg when that tone started bending." She flips her eyes at him, she turns up the corners of her mouth. Then they both know.

"Yes," thinks Mrs. Martin, "his tone is good. But I'm sorry, Shorty Baker's tone was much prettier. Though I have to say Marsalis is cuter."

Jazz music is always in the process of becoming itself. So is a gig. We are into the engagement now. The early jitters are gone. The blues is in trouble tonight. It's time to vaccinate ourselves and our audience with a nice, hot, slow blues. In D. Me on the microphone: "Time for some blues." Various replies: "Okay, yeah, well alright." Veal deep in the pocket for three choruses by himself. Soon to be joined by Eric tinkling up high. Homey in the center of a good ol' country-ass blues. No thinking. This is past thought. Reflexes trained to respond by countless hours of on-bandstand experiences, of stylizing off-bandstand interactions.

Warm Daddy pouring soul through his horn, locked in mortal combat with the blues. *"You better watch yourself!" "There it is!" "Say that!" "Have mercy!" "You mean that!"* That's us. Standing to the side or in the shadows, but participating in every phrase. He plays also to impress us. We encourage each other, we listen and anticipate with such purity that we imagine ourselves to be . . .

"Warm Daddy!" Nathan shocks himself by standing and shouting this most basic of responses to Wes Anderson's alto and the playing of some blues. Most basic because it could also take place in the famed house of Tokyo's Kabuki theater, where the most recent Danjuro in a centuries-long line of actors bearing that name is acclaimed with fervor at the elegant execution of an expressive maneuver. "Danjuro!"

Here comes Pine Cone with the trombone. Pure D jazz blues, Cone style. Each instrument will whip the butt of the blues from another perspective. T Bone knows this: "Play it low. Get down low where the blues lives. This boy can play some blues, I know that." He is comfortable now, hopeful that his date with Adrienne will go past eleven P.M. She loves the blues, too! "Did you hear how he played that plunger, baby? Look, now, that's some bad-ass shit you just heard. Excuse my language, but that's the only way to say it. Shit! How you think I got my nickname? I know about the trombone."

The Deacon plays two sensual choruses on the low, low clarinet. *"Leave something for me, Deke,"* I say, *"leave me something."* Now, trumpet held high, I am trying to swing, am swinging. Me, Veal, Homey, and Eric develop ideas and play, play with the blues, together, each negotiating concord from his own perspective.

Mrs. Martin claps on two and four, and her wig slips slightly left of center. She is happy. "I like that drummer. But he ain't no Sam Woodyard. Marsalis, well, he need to stick to playing classical music. Any one random chorus of any trumpeter of my day contains more soul than everything he has ever played. Even this tune I'm clappin' on."

I hit a high one and hold it. Lips swollen, cut by teeth, head bursting, heart straining; it must be held longer. Past the point of pain. This note is for Nathan. He respects the desire to make something good, great. Mr. Fernandez's band claps and hollers for that note. Nathan, he says nothing. Only runs his tongue along his lips and thinks, "That must hurt even him." He is more than right. It hurts, but it feels good. Better than the hurt because we are grown men engaged in (mere) child's play. Romping without fear. Playing the blues. The jazz blues.

My solo is over. Now all four horns come forward and the entire band girds for one final assault. When on death ground, play. On the edge of their seats, those who have come tonight realize that we are about to witness once again the unequivocal defeat of bad times.

"Not too many fast notes."

"Let me play high and fast."

"Slap the bass."

"Damn, the horns are dragging, let me bolster them up with some rolls."

"What is Wynton going to play here?"

"Let's play this riff."

"Okay, Cone, here's my response."

"He's answering Cone, let me harmonize it." The Deacon shouts up high on the clarinet.

"I'll just lay out."

That's us talking to each other, a continuous negotiation designed to use the full power, intelligence, and feeling of the band. Every instrument comments on the limitations of the other instruments, but together we fire unlimited commentary at the blues. Like the litany of witnesses called to testify against the guilty in a court of law. To indict him with himself. *"Ain't that a bitch?"* We step forward together to convict the blues with the blues. But we are jazz musicians, so we proceed not just as witnesses but also as lawyers trained in precedent and the intricacies of indictment. Guilty as charged. No loophole or plea bargain, justice will be served this evening.

"Let's build it up."

"Don't let the intensity down."

"Not too loud."

"Leave room for Wes."

"Yes, yes, yass." Deep in the groove with all cylinders open, we take the song out to a crescendo of applause.

"Now that's jazz, gotdammit, that is jazz music!" T Bone springs from his seat, sneaking a look at Adrienne's own rising posterior.

"You see how hard they were workin'. That's what I like. I hate a man who's lazy," Adrienne hints at him.

"Who you talkin' about, baby?"

"My uncle."

We take our audience through the many movements inspired by and implied in the entire history of jazz. Complexity of up-tempo counterpoints and virtuoso passages, emotional ebb and flow of extended pieces, sensuousness of slow songs, dance-beat motion of grooves, and the timeless joy of New Orleans music. This is the end of the twentieth, but we play jazz, real jazz, for the public.

Mr. Fernandez's students are restless now. Two and one-half hours of swing is enough for many of them. They are ready to go home and watch some TV. Not Nathan, though, he clings to every phrase, ever deeper into the groove of each swinging moment. Time has revealed the truth to his fellow students. Long after their superficial involvement has ended, long after the last echo of "Huh, Nathan?" Nathan is still swinging—harder. They are tired.

Yes, our musical conversations will soon end, on a stage that has resembled in the last two hours an altar, field of battle, library, court of law, late-night bedroom, playground, and so many streets of a modern metropolis. We will once again have participated in an exorcism of the blues by playing the blues, the jazz blues.

Mrs. Martin has particularly enjoyed the selections that most remind her of her youth. "Well, at least they are trying to play, they do play a wide range of music. But not as good as in my day. A five-course meal of mediocre food is just as bad as a one. That's what I say," if only to herself.

T Bone's arm rests comfortably on Adrienne's shoulder, and even though she is unfamiliar with a lot of this music, she likes T Bone's involvement in it. He is different from the other men she knows.

This is me: "Thank you very much, ladies and gentlemen. We hope that you have enjoyed yourselves. Take care, and have a very good night. Bye-bye." The rhythm section keeps swinging, as the horns leave the stage playing. Todd and I keep on playing, speaking to each other in the language of jazz. Now the whole band comes offstage, Veal, Homey, and Eric singing and clapping, having left bass, drums, and piano behind. Our audience rises to its feet in recognition of the resounding victory they have enjoyed. We continue the music backstage, grown men deeply engaged in child's play. Like astronauts floating in space.

"Let's go bow." Out we go once again, over wires into an arena of com-

bat now worn and smoldering from the heat of tonight's engagement. Glowing in the warmth of goodwill extended by all those who came to turn the blues back, heads down, we are glad to see only shoes in a display of thanks and humility that reminds us of the Japanese custom—the greater the man, the lower the bow. So we bow lower as if it will elevate us in the eyes of those who have participated this evening. We are Americans.

Back out, offstage, cold and dark. The playing is over. And like those schoolkids squeezing the last second out of recess, we are together, musicians and audience, in wanting to savor more. The applause grows louder. We walk onto the stage, swinging a New Orleans parade march. But this is Topeka, or San Francisco, or Peoria, or Raleigh. Then the unusual happens. *"Should we go?"* I ask Todd. *"Why not,"* the Deacon replies. Out into the cold night air we plunge like a big, many-headed caterpillar. Warmth of the sound challenging the chill. Our audience ecstatic in the recreation of a ritual as old as water, the procession. No longer do we see red exit signs from the stage. Only streetlights and car lights and the gleaming eyes of those glad to be reunited with their oldest self.

Everybody loves a parade. Mr. Fernandez's band is out there stepping. They know something about marching. Nathan has his horn out, joining the band. He even knows the tune, "The Second Line." T Bone blows a whistle from Adrienne's keychain, delivering a lecture, between toots, on the history and meaning of the New Orleans jazz parade. "Ouch! You're stepping on my feet"—that's Adrienne. "Oh, baby, I'm sorry, I just got carried away." She gazes at him.

Even Mrs. Martin is outside stepping with dignity, happy to be moving to the jazz blues. "They should have known that the dance hall is the place for jazz. Or a parade. Look at how much fun people are having. I sure wish Chester was alive to see this. He wouldn't believe this. He thought jazz died with him. They not as good as Chester and them was. But at least they are playing jazz—real jazz."

Grown-ups engaged in (mere) child's play. Up one block and down another, horns held high, sound of percussion and brass once used to strike fear in the enemy now signaling the joy of the blues' ass well whipped. Cymbals and clarinet like the procession of musicians through the streets on a Chinese holiday. We are that, too. We are Americans. We play the blues. Grooving around a long block, trumpet cutting through the night like a fog light at an airport, people jumping and smiling, two policemen watching, knowing some city ordinance is being broken, but not caring. Herlin Riley, master of the New Orleans drum cadence, plays a washboard in the street as if it is a full set of drums and cymbals onstage. Warm Daddy riffs with the steady beat of windshield wipers turning back the rain. Veal on Cone's trombone tailgates like a slippery pig between unseasoned arms. The Deacon blows hot wind up high through the clarinet like air howling through a slightly opened car window, fast notes cascading. Cone's tuba roars like small units of perfectly timed thunder or the steps of Gulliver in the land of the Lilliputians. Nathan does the best he can.

We parade back into the hall. This could be any point on the long and distinguished time line of the oh-so-human search for a lasting and profound happiness. But this is the end of the twentieth century. We settle for the temporary feeling of profound happiness. Two and one-half to three hours of jazz music. Enemy was the blues laid low in public by grown-ups engaged in (mere) child's play. We are jazzmen. Playing the blues still, the jazz blues. Eight o'clock P.M. All over the world. Forever.

T BONE IS EXCITED. He is sure that Adrienne has enjoyed herself, and now perhaps they will return to her apartment and engage in the world's favorite activity. They pull up at 315 Hillside Avenue. Get out of the car. Walk to the door. She kisses his cheek, tells him good night, and then, the door closes. He walks slowly to his car, turns back every now and then to no avail, gets in and drives away. Pops in a tape of Sonny Stitt playing "I Can't

Get Started with You." Says to himself, "Three weeks of my party money. Damn. She sure is fine." Listens to some more Stitt. "Yeah, Sonny, I know. Yep. At least I got a date. Oh yeah, I will be calling back tomorrow." He too is a jazzman, he plays the blues in his mind.

Mrs. Martin goes home on the bus. She has been saving for months to attend tonight's skirmish. She lives in the Hill housing projects with two granddaughters and a grandson. Her daughter is there, too. Her no-good son-in-law, however, is nowhere to be found. She opens the door only to see her grandchildren, ages eight, eleven, and twelve, sitting in front of the television, watching women in drawers assume semipornographic poses while men with hands on genitalia chant rhymed doggerel to an incessant beat. Young sensibilities slowly destroyed by the alpha-wave onslaught of ignorance efficiently delivered to the learning centers of the brain. For the monetary gain of others, whom they would never meet. Others that don't even like them.

"Hey, Grandma, how was that show you saw?"

"Great. Those young men are the greatest musicians I ever heard. Even better than Duke Ellington and Count Basie. You should have heard their trombonist. And the way they dressed. And Marsalis, well, not only is he handsome, he plays that classical music, too. You all should come with me next time, if Grandma can get the money. Lawd, and did they play some blues. They even had your old grandma out in the street marchin', honey. And you know when I come home from work, I'm too tired to be doin' any marchin'."

She goes on, but they are not listening. Minds go on frying in visual projections of the purest ignorance and worst intentions. They do not respect the woman who sustains their lives. They are the uninitiated. Mere children, victims of grown-up play. Mrs. Martin makes them turn off the television and go to bed. She is tired. She goes into her bedroom and describes the concert to the only person interested. Chester. He smiles to her from a photograph taken long ago. She must rise early in the morning to cook breakfast, send the kids to school, and then go to work. She is tired. Enemy is the blues on high ground.

Mr. Fernandez is about to come backstage with his band to take photos and talk music. These pictures will end up on one of the bulletin boards in the band room, perhaps beneath some anecdote to inspire practicing.

The band members are elated because Nathan has had a chance to play with his idols. We are sweaty and tired, but we feel good. We have played three hours of hot, sweet, soulful jazz music with intelligence and skill. Participated in a ritual, as old as man and woman, made new in New Orleans at the turn of the twentieth century. We know that this is the end of the twentieth century, and we are still jazzmen. It is our birthright. Grown-ups proudly engaged in (mere) child's play. Playing the blues. The jazz blues. We will bask in the temporary feeling of a profound happiness. The blues, however badly beaten, will return. So will we.

4. RIFF

I t's like the end of a hard day of physical work. Before I entered high school, a fawly of mine and I were janitors at the school for the summer. We painted ceilings, moved desks, put new light bulbs in every classroom. You never realize how many light bulbs there are in a big school until you put one in every fixture. Then you never forget. My father always told me, "Son, learn how to work a job."

This was reinforced musically by my experience with Art Blakey. Night in and night out he played with the same intensity and desire. An old man, on the road for forty-odd years, putting his foot into the ass of the young and unengaged. In the band we say, Let's rededicate ourselves to the swing. Every night. So when we stand before our audience, we can face them without shame. We are doing the best that we can, all the time. When the music sounds sad, it's an accident and not a habit. Playing the gig always gives us energy. It feels good. We're ready for some more something.

WHENEVER YOU SEE old, cross-shaped hot and cold faucet handles in an old, mildewy, thick-green-painted, ugly-wallpaper-having dressing room, you know you are truly on the circuit. Only one of them will work, and it won't be the hot. If by some miracle the hot does work, it will scald you and no cold will be available. Plus, the mirror won't be above the sink, it'll be on the opposite wall, so to shave you have to run back and forth from the

sink to the mirror. The toilet always features that hard brown paper that leaves you greatly dissatisfied.

In all but the most wonderful instances the only thing you can do in a room like this is sit and think. After a fiery trombone solo, Cone cools off with a towel over his head. He has to let the heat from the last set's ideas slowly dissipate. That's how Cone is, patient.

WES LOVES to have his smoke alone. And we love for him to have that smoke alone. Wes has wanted to be a jazz musician his entire life. Now he is, so you better not mess with him about his smoking. 'Cause he sure won't mess with you.

Many times after a gig you want to be alone and let the experience settle in. If you haven't played well, you have to figure out what was going on. And if you truly sounded sad, you are almost too embarrassed to face the other cats. They'll say, "Hey, man, you alright? What's happening, man?" Or, "Whew! I don't know."

Then you say, "I'm sorry, y'all. I know I wasn't playin' shit."

And they say, "Boy, that's the truth. But neither was I."

Wes'll adjust his reed, too, that's part of playing a reed instrument. From the time we played together in funk bands as teenagers, Branford drove me crazy fiddling with his reed. I'd be thinking he wouldn't come in

with the next part because his reed wouldn't be right. Wes, too. If his reed is not right, he will slap his nose and ears like he's trying to brush away a fly. He doesn't like bugs. At outdoor concerts at night the lights attract bugs in droves, and poor Wes slaps away at himself all night long.

OUR ROAD MANAGER, Matt Dillon, is called the Major because he orders everyone around. "Get in the van!" We laugh. He loves to hold forth in the dressing room on the latest scheme he has concocted for our enjoyment. He calls everyone baby—"Come on, baby." Except when he's in his ordering mode. In foreign countries he pretends to be a native speaker trying out his English: "Get in zee van, Monsour!" He is tenacious on the basketball court and is not above fouling you or cheating to win. He loves to call band meetings, which we hate. People genuinely like him because he knows how to have a good time without feeling guilty.

This intermission conversation forced him to listen, however, instead of holding forth. David Robinson came into the dressing room to let us

know what the deal was. "Man, what are y'all doing? I didn't leave Houston to hear this kind of shit. I come to work to swing. Every set. Are you only a second-half band? If y'all don't want to play, let me know so I can go back to my room and put on some Trane. I'm not getting paid enough to listen to nothing like that. Let's get on a vibe. Give these people some jazz music. Let them know what we are about." Gotdammit.

VEAL HAS GATHERED Herlin, Stephen Scott (who played piano with us for a while), and me to discuss the state of our swing. "Hey, bruh. I don't know if y'all are aware of the fact that we haven't been swinging. At all. I'm not saying nobody is trying, but it ain't happening." He is very clear about what needs to be done to address this problem. Play softer, concentrate, play together. Stop choosing poor directions for the music to go in, stop being too self-centered and hoarding the swing, stop being 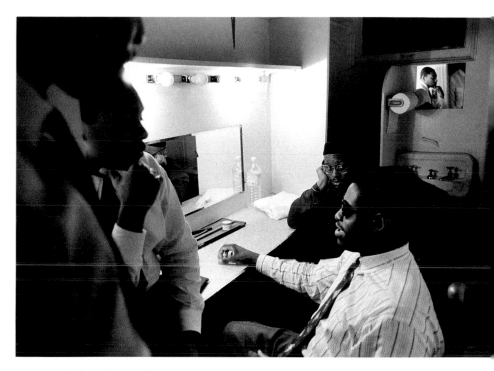 unspontaneous and afraid to trust our ears and reflexes. Not swinging comes to a head now and then.

One time Veal spoke up because cats wouldn't let him take any solos. "Man, I want to solo just like you. You know how you all feel when you take a solo? That's how I wanna feel." But what Veal talks about most is playing with intelligence. The unamplified bass is the softest instrument on the bandstand. When we play too loud, it can't be heard and can't participate in the dialogue. Veal listens intently all night and plays things for us to interact with. When we overplay, it hurts his feelings. He hates to see the potential for fresh music destroyed by clichés. To him unintelligent playing is like having a big stain on your tie. You spend more time looking at the stain than at the tie.

WHEN DESI comes to the gig with Wes IV, we sandwich him in the kitchen of the Village Vanguard with some blues. We call him Quad. He wants to play the drums like his grandfather. Most of us come from musical families, and we loved going to gigs when we were younger. Not for the music, just the ambience. Being exposed to the swing gives kids another understanding. You can tell by his face that Quad digs the swing. Just like his momma.

ED ARRENDELL, my business manager, is largely responsible for our being able to stay on the road. 'Cause I have no sense or liking for money matters at all. He teases me and says I am the Bank of Skayne (my nickname), because so many people call the office for money. He brings his son Chad to the gigs. Chad wants to play the trumpet, so I play "Sesame Street" for him. The trumpet always needs new recruits.

Ed has an MBA from Harvard, but he is not above putting his foot in some behind if need be. "Let me pull my watch off," he'll say, "and we can settle this in the final court."

Once we got pulled over by a roadblock of about fifteen policemen looking for Negro bank robbers in Culpeper County, Virginia. They approached our car, guns and shotguns drawn. Ed gets out of the car cussin' and acting a fool. It was beautiful.

HERLIN AND PATRICIA have five children. A "handful" as Homey likes to
say. Raynice is their newest and "last,"
as he also likes to say. When she was
born, we were in Princeton, New Jer-
sey. We toasted Homey and then went
out and swang. Two days later he
caught the first plane out. Upon his
return Homey talked so much about his
baby we all wanted to see her. We did-

n't have to wait long. Herlin convinced Pat to bring her to San Francisco.
Raynice was then only one month old. She is what we call twice beautiful,
because in addition to being cute she has the blessing of charm and a lov-
ing personality. But don't think that means you can boss her around. Her
tweaky little voice will tell you "I don't like that" in a minute.

LIL' WYNTON AND SIMEON came backstage to profile with Daddy. I stole the term "jazz blues" from them. Wynton likes to play the drums or beat on anything handy. He always plays the same rhythm—$\frac{4}{4}$ ♩. ♩. ♩♩. ♩. ♩—with plenty of feeling. Then Simeon picks up anything that resembles a horn and pretends to play the trumpet—do-dodee, do-do-dooeee. That is the jazz blues according to them, incantation and percussion. They love the New Orleans standard "Bourbon Street Parade." Simeon says, "Daddy, play Dee-Dee-Dee." That means pull my horn out and play so that he can pantomime and Wynton can beat on some furniture. They love to pillow fight, but Simeon quits whenever he gets hit.

They also like to hear scary stories at bedtime. I know they are jazzmen in spirit because when I pull a book out, they say, "No, no, no. Say it with your mouth, Daddy, with your mouth." That means, "Make up something that we will like." Furthermore, as they become increasingly lost attempting to follow the plot, they cosign every pause with an "Uh-hum" or "Yes" or "And then what did he do?" Then they fall asleep. Here they affect their noblest pose.

AN IMPORTANT EVENT in the development of a young jazz musician is being sent back home to woodshed. It has happened to all of us. We don't like it, but how we deal with it often determines the nature of our future involvement with this music. Even the great Charlie Parker was dismissed unceremoniously from the bandstand by the throwing of a Jo Jones cymbal. At him! That's why Farid is not downcast at having to go home and shed. He'll be mad for a little while, then he'll get it together. Like we all have had to do.

THEN, OF COURSE, THERE IS THE ROAD. You miss your family and loved ones. Your suit is wrinkled; room service never came and you are starving; you didn't bring enough drawers; the shower in the hotel has only cold water; we haven't sold any tickets to tonight's gig; you have a box of bad reeds; you had another terrible argument with your old lady; the cats in the band are getting on your nerves; your favorite tie is lost; you left your music on the bus; you can't find a place to get a good haircut; you were late for the gig; you are tired of playing what you've been playing; you keep thinking about the worst things that have ever happened to you; plus, you tripped on a wire walking off the stage and banged your knee.

Then you find yourself in an ugly, hot dressing room with a bottle of orange juice from concentrate. You sit down with your horn and say, "Whew!" Enemy is the blues on high ground. Foot embedded deeply.

5. AMEN CADENCE

love the time right after the gig almost as much as playing. Then I meet people and get new ideas and inspiration. It could be someone's accent, a woman's earrings, the way someone looks at me, the way people hold each other's hands. One time someone told me, "I put on your album 'Hot-house Flowers' when I'm in the afterglow." That phrase said so much to me, I wrote a song entitled "In the Afterglow."

What I really love about meeting people we have played for is the range of personalities. Some people slept through the concert, others just came to see what the audience was wearing. There are people who love the music and say, "Man, please sign these twenty-two CDs for me. Please." Others go, "Lord, when is this gonna be over? I hate this kinda music." All of that is a part of playing. One person will say, "Oh, my father used to play trumpet, and he loved Roy Eldridge. I'm glad to see y'all bringing jazz back." Another will say, "Take this picture with me, Quinton, because if I know somebody famous, Toni might be impressed and give me her phone number. Here, write 'To my main man, Rendell, from high school.' Yeah, man, you alright with me. Thanks, Quint." That's the beauty of it. If everybody was one way, it wouldn't be nearly as hip.

"I JUST GOT YOUR NEW CD. Thank you. My wife and I got married to your music."

"Yeah, man, I don't really like that jazz. But I like what you're playing, you, Herb Alpert, Kenny G., and Grover."

"I don't like the stuff you had on, you need to talk more to the people, the band don't smile enough."

EVERYBODY COMES FOR what they think is going on. An older, very dignified person may be embarrassed. "I've never asked anybody for an autograph. I'm sixty-two years old, but I like you because you're clean-cut."

An old cat daddy in a white straw hat or a fedora will come up, clean and fine down to the polish on his fingernails and his patent leather shoes. "Yeah, Mawsellis, I love what you're playing, baby. I been watching you since you came out with Blakey. I just wanta tell you that you're my man. I don't care what they say about you. And you keep talking, too! Don't you let them shut you up. They don't want you to be strong. Don't want you tellin' the truth. That's the truth you're talking, and the truth hurts people. Black and white. Yeah, baby. Boy, your daddy must be proud. I'm gonna tell you something, I like that boy on the bass, too. Boy's got one of those big ol' oak tree tones. Where do you find these boys at? I didn't know that existed anymore, things so messed up and crazy out here. Even my niece loves you. I have to tell her, 'That boy's a musician, baby. Watch out.' Sign this, man; yeah, put your name right here. To Berniece, B, e, r, niece. Yeah, that's it. You come from a good family upbringing. You're not talking all that street trash and ignorance. You my man. Don't lose that common touch, man. Let's get this picture. Come on here and take this picture of me and Mawsell."

Two skycaps and their girlfriends show up because we have given them complimentary tickets. Earlier in the day we were in the airport and one said to the other, "Hey man, that's Marcel. He plays the horn. You know. He won one of the awards, an Emmy." The other said, "Who?" So I went over and heard, "Man, I was just telling André about how you won those Academy Awards. He didn't even know who you was."

"Man, you know I heard of this man."

"No, you didn't. You didn't even know he plays on the *Tonight Show*."

IN A BIG CROWD you just sign, you can't talk. Whenever you're surrounded by a pile of women, men will be on the side saying, "We know you love this." But you won't meet any of these women. There are too many, you won't be able to talk to one of them. Plus, when you're finished signing, all of the food is gone! So you go home hungry.

AT COLLEGE GIGS I'll hear, "Man, I like your music. I study to it. Classical and jazz. I heard you like to play basketball, man; I should do some work on you tomorrow. When are you all leaving?"

"You know, I started getting clean 'cause I saw you on your album covers. I don't know if I'm as clean as you, though. But I do know my shoes are badder than yours."

"I used to play the horn, man, but I had to give it up, it's too hard to find a job. I'm a communications major now, but I still pick up my horn every now and then. Man, I love 'Black Codes from the Underground.' When you gonna make another one like that?"

"How's your brother doing?"

"Man, write this autograph for my girlfriend. We had a little argument, that's why she's not here. I want to get back in tight with her. Write

something sweet. Her name is Patrice, but I call her Patsy. Put 'To Patsy' on there."

"You're much cuter in person than on the albums." Giggle, giggle, giggle. "My daddy loves your music. Are you married?" Giggle. "I'm a musician and I read all of your interviews. I don't agree with everything you say, but I respect your opinions. Why aren't you married? That's too personal, huh? Well, what are y'all doing later? My boyfriend, Ronnie, loves jazz. He had to work tonight. Make him jealous and write on this." Giggle. "Thank you. I didn't realize it would be this easy to get backstage." Giggle.

"I think that twentieth-century classical music can present states of emotional complexity with much more accuracy than jazz."

"What jazz are you talking about?"

"I don't know . . . all of it."

Uh-huh.

"Standard Time Volume 2 has one of the dumbest CD covers ever. It's disrespectful to women. I thought you had more dignity than that. But y'all still sounded good."

BACKSTAGE after a gig is an occasion for heavy profiling. People have put on their finery to hear us play and meet us. This makes me proud. So I pay close attention to everything that is said.

"My husband, Greg, and I came to hear you play on our first date. We named our cat Wynton."

"Our children were born to the sound of your music."

"Conceived or born?" I ask.

"Both," they say.

"Um-hmmm."

"How can I get a break in the music business? I want to be up there like you."

"Break to a practice room."

"Pass this tape on to someone at a record company. I can sing, too!"

"Okay." I smile and take the tape.

"Man, y'all weren't playing shit. I wasted my money. You should give me a refund."

"Speak to this man. He handles all complaints." I send them to Todd Williams, who is so nice they are embarrassed.

"How high can you play?"

"This high."

"I didn't hear anything."

"Man, all the dogs in this neighborhood are going crazy."

"You have the sexiest lips. Can I have just one sweet, juicy kiss? And now a big hug?"

I tell the young musicians standing around, "Practice."

"Yeah, man, I never thought I could see nobody put on a plaid jacket and make it hip, but you pulled it off tonight, Skayne. Get this picture, man. People say I look like you."

"You know I look way better than you, man."

We both look in the mirror and laugh.

"You look too skinny, child. Next time you're in town, come to my house for a good home-cooked meal."

ANOTHER RULE OF BACKSTAGE is, the camera never works. Everybody's smile has melted three minutes ago and someone is still saying, "Wait for the red light, Emily, the red light. Now press the black button.

The black button. No, the other one. Yeah, try it again. Press it. Let me see it."

But still I love being photographed with families. First, families mostly look the same, so they're cute in a uniform sort of way. Second, I love the thought of being in their family album. It'll be with the pictures they have of all the concerts they've gone to. They'll say, "That's the picture we took when we saw Marsalis."

I love to see the pride of a mother or father whose child plays for us backstage. We always tell youngsters to bring their horns. We listen to them play and comment on it even if just for five minutes.

"What do you want to play?" That's me.

"I don't know." That's Johnny.

"Play that song you drive me crazy with." That's Momma.

Finally a little music trickles out of the horn. I always say something good and then offer constructive criticism. Young musicians are very sensitive. You have to be a good judge of character to levy certain criticisms, and even if you are sometimes you make a mistake. Then, too, sometimes one of the world's great trumpeters or trumpet teachers will come backstage and I will have the opportunity to get a lesson myself.

Every year Gunther Schuller drives from Sandpoint, Idaho, to Spokane, Washington, and we sit up all night and discuss music. He has written two of the finest books on jazz music. I love the challenge of conversing with him. He adjudicated my audition to enter Tanglewood in 1979, and I have tremendous respect for his opinions. Even if we disagree. That he takes the time to come see us makes me feel good. That's how I feel about our audiences.

"COME GET THIS PICTURE with the parents of my band members. This is our booster club. That's why the program is successful."

"You know, Duke played this theater in 1968. The Rex is a great theater. So did Louis Armstrong. They ruled Buenos Aires. I was here, I know. People were all in the front row crying."

"I didn't know y'all had this kind of scene around you. This is hip. Where did you find Herlin?"

"What is the story behind your trumpet?"

"It's made by Dave Monette. He lives outside of Portland, Oregon."

"Is the mouthpiece built in?"

"Yes."

"Did you help design it?"

"Nope. He channels the design through Sheldon, his cat."

"Oh. Do you mind taking a picture? With the horn, too? Can I hold it?"

Okay, smile now, don't leave me out here smiling by myself.

"How's your brother? Do you ever play with him?"

"I was on his last album."

"Do you get along?"

"Do you have brothers and sisters?"

"Yes."

"Do you get along?"

"Sometimes."

Well.

AFTER THE CONCERT the people working in the hall are anxious to go home. Sometimes they tell the people who want to come backstage, "He won't sign autographs." I always stay until the last autograph is signed. The old musicians in New Orleans always say, "Stay with the people. Stay with the people." I'm glad to be a small part of people's lives. It's a privilege to be on the road. I could be home in Kenner, Louisiana, gigless. I learned this watching my father for so many years. I also remember meeting the great trumpeter Clark Terry when I was fifteen years old. He got up early the next morning to hear me play the Brandenburg Concerto No. 2 with the

New Orleans Symphony. He also sent me a postcard from Europe during
one of his tours. That kind of stuff encourages you and stays with you your
whole life. So I stay until the last person.

"We finally got this camera to work. We know you're tired, but can we
please get one more shot with you?"

"Sign this 'To Yolanda and Zack.' "

THANKS FOR COMING OUT.

6. SWEET REFRAIN

They will tell you that romance is a matter of the imagination. Laugh at this silliness. Romance is an intense relationship with reality. A reality so hidden by the many layers of traditional misconceptions and compromises as to seem fantasy.

PAIN IS IN THE WORLD. But there is a tenderness, a sweetness, a lovingness in our interactions. It is us at our best.

Recall those first moments of pure terror. In-Out, In-Out, In, gasping for the first breath. Wonder at the warmth of a touch both foreign and native. It is foreign, it titillates. It is native, it comforts. Then comes recognition: this is our first romance. We draw the milk slowly then quickly, greedily, for life depends on our getting as much as possible, as soon as possible, this ritual the only point of clarity in a world of uncertainty. As we cling to her breast, we are the insecure made secure. In-Out, In-Out, in a trance, the ancient impulse takes over, and long after our hunger is satiated, we hold on.

Yes, we are dependent and helpless, but we bring a desire to be loved and an unquestioning acceptance of what is given, an honest helplessness that inspires benevolence. This makes her want to give more even when it hurts. She knows that our love is the purest and truest, based on recognition of her person, and accurate because she is all that we can perceive of humankind. From this time, all of our senses are trained to detect the possibility of romance. The chance to recognize and interact with a sweetness,

a tenderness, a lovingness. Pain is in the world, but if we are lucky, through her kindness we experience the sweetness of life. And we never forget. If we are unlucky, well . . . we have a bad time. Yes, a very bad time.

It is said that hardened veterans, wounded in combat, will cry one name, "Mama." It is the same in almost every language. And its utterance evokes the same feeling, "lovingkindness." She is our first teacher. In-Out, In-Out, like great artists who can raise ancient solutions from the valley of the been-dead and instruct a wayward people, this mother's feeling translates the experiences of generations of people long gone from this world of chaos. We will gladly accept her solutions. We have none.

Out into the world of chaos we pop, disoriented by the individuality that will one day be the source of our greatest pride. Through recognition of her we discover ourselves. Through us, she discovers another portion of herself. We are now in our grace period. Mother and child discovering the world again and for the first time. This has a special glow.

Actually, it's cute. A child cannot choose. Every discovery is a triumph. But a thing is only new once. If we wish to continue a romance with the world of feeling, we must make sense of our sensual discoveries. Develop an understanding that takes us further away from dependence on her. Give her the opportunity to perform the most heroic of romantic acts, grant us the freedom to choose what we will romance, accept us as ourselves. This is our birthright.

Deeper into the world we plunge. In-Out, In-Out, In-Out in 3/4 time. That is our heartbeat. With the reading of every book, looking at every flower, meeting of every person, eating of every meal, we learn something of the grandeur of the world. For sure, we have many unsavory and bitter experiences, but these always lead us, if we are lucky and optimistic, to a greater appreciation of what we like. If we are unlucky and pessimistic, well . . .

We romance the world. A stick becomes a boat rushing down the rapids of a bathtub. A trail of ants becomes the whole Roman legion come to capture your kingdom. A bowl of spaghetti becomes the hair of your worst friend's mother. Discovery, recognition, understanding, in 3/4 time we play. And playing is indeed romantic. Out of your mouth can flow insults, compliments, jokes, profanities, nonsense, whispers, or plain conversation. You love it. It continues. The titillation of the new like your first encounter with a strawberry or a scrambled egg, and the comfort of the routine like your favorite meal. And always she loves you, that is the foundation of your courage to explore and develop. She is your safety net. Even in failure, you are still loved.

Now, however, you have many intimates. From father and father-like figures who help expand your conception of the possible to the many like-gendered friends with whom you share more immediate concerns, the In and Out of learning and acting on knowledge becomes your favorite pastime. On top of strong shoulders watching the parade, learning to catch a baseball on one hop, telling your young secrets, fighting after school, looking up skirts on stairs, and even butt whippings after intentional or unintentional misjudgments— romance.

And, of course, having something good to eat. A good, hot, home-cooked supper represents more than just basic survival. Even when you argue at the table, it is romantic, prepared with love and style. They say that the greatest chefs are men. But we know that the best meals are to be had in the many homes presided over by her who has the greatest stake in our development. This is the end of the twentieth century. You will hear that men and women are the same. It is not yet true.

"Man, my mama cook way better than your mama."

"Man, I been at your house, I had that old bland food that she call cooking."

"Bland, you think that's blander than that sad potato salad your momma make? That taste like paste, man."

"You talking about paste, I saw your mama putting some real paste into that nasty-ass soup she make."

"At least she know what soup is."

This is the only circumstance under which a negative reference to Momma will be tolerated. Only because you know that sooner or later you will return to each other's homes bowing, cheesing, and scraping for whatever is on the stove. Then, outside, you will exchange views on who received the worst behind whipping for messing up.

"My daddy caught me talking back to my momma. He lit me up."

"My momma saw me hanging with Gus and them after she told me not to. I couldn't sit down for two days, man."

Strange, but true, you equate the punishment with a concern for your development.

Now, discipline is not fashionable, perhaps for the best. This is the end of the twentieth century. You will hear that men and women are the same. But not on holidays. Or if you are sick. Then you are reacquainted with the lovingkindness of your first romance. If you are lucky.

In-Out, In-Out. in 2/4 time. There is a new feeling in the air. We suddenly detect it, and our response is immediate.

"Can I walk you home?"

"Why?"

"I just want to talk."

"About what?"

"The dance next week."

"No."

Well, at least she looked at me when she said no. This is beautiful, because we both can choose—the chance for ultimate romance, almost. Almost, because the blood that rushes through our veins is too new, too hot, to do anything but excite. It is unfamiliar, unsettling, and uncomfortable. But we love it. Now the hair and the clothes for the eyes. The various talcs and powders for the smell. The playing of slow, sensuous songs for the hearing. The chewing of gums and mints for the tasting. The cultivation of sweet and provocative language for the mind—yes, that is a sense, too.

"Do you know what this is?"

"Who drew that?"

"Me."

"It's an angel."

"Guess again."

"I know that's an angel."

"No, baby, it's you."

"Me?"

"Would you like to go to the dance with me next week?"

"Maybe."

That's better than no. And so it begins. In-Out, In-Out in 2/4 time, the sparring of would-be lovers, young lovers. Discovery, recognition, perhaps understanding, a whole world of turmoil to rummage through in search of a kindness, a sweetness, a lovingness. The final stage of titillation in this new world is in the way you touch each other. After this will be comfort, or disillusion. But it is never one touch. Many at once. We touch each slowly, then quickly, greedily, for life depends on our getting as much as possible, as soon as possible. This touching crowns a life of touches. We put our entire insecure selves into it, seeking to be made secure as we once were on our mother's breast and in her arms. This touching is a point of clarity in a world made uncertain by hormones and fads. So we touch and search with the fervor of a treasure hunter on the lips of his X-marks-the-spot. As if we would turn the new to old in an instant of rapid repetition. In-Out, In-Out, in 2/4 time up-tempo, too quickly the song has ended. We cling to each other long after our hunger is satiated, in a trance.

If we possessed understanding, we would know that a thing is only

new once. We would know that the facade of a thing gives no hint of what lurks behind. We would not be fooled by the immediate intensity of the new. But we are too young yet. Blinded by the heat of the encounter, we will happily settle for discovery and recognition in 2/4 time. Understanding may come later. Perhaps then we will realize that sustained intensity equals ecstasy. And sustained could mean a lifetime, or many lifetimes.

And if we are truly observant, sustained could mean the lifetime of a moment. You see, romance is on its own time. One second of it contains all of it. Like a drop of water.

Yes, we are mere children engaged in grown-up's play. We play with a fire that has burned brightly even before the time of Prometheus. It can illuminate or it can burn.

We think no longer of our mothers. We will leap into other, more accepting arms. Experience will be our only teacher, because we must now rebel against what we love. Leave love to find love. In-Out, In-Out. Days and nights filled with thoughts of this titillation again, in 2/4 time. The memories of these adolescent passions have more intensity than the acts themselves.

A thing is only new once. But we will do our best to make this once last as long as possible.

"You don't understand," we tell those who knew us before we knew ourselves. "Pay for us to play." And they will, if possible, because this is our grace period. In a way it's cute. But not as cute as when you were a baby. You have more choices; some are grave. If we possessed understanding we would know that though rebellion is a sign of choice, it is not the only sign. You might rebel yourself out of being you, in search of a tenderness, a sweetness, a lovingness. Not understanding that God offers pleasure as divine revelation, the devil proffers it to deceive. The possibility of a pain-filled deception makes our young love serious. She who has raised us will not experience this pain for us. It is ours, inescapable. And we hate it.

Pain disciplines our spirit if we are lucky and optimistic. If we are unlucky and pessimistic, it kills. Not the permanent In-Out, In-Out, final-gasp death. But worse, no eating, no laughing, no bathing, no talking. No, pain is in the world, and romance will not wait for the broken-hearted. It continues like so many clocks, look if you want to know what time it is. If you don't, it keeps ticking. In-Out, In-Out, In-Out, In-Out.

Don't be fooled. Romance is an intense relationship with reality. A reality so cloaked by the many-layered tapestry of traditional misconceptions and compromises as to seem fantasy. Romance the mind? Many will choose to romance the behind. And will be behind.

But save your breath, nothing will separate young fools from their misconceptions. This is our grace period. Besides, it is fun, mostly. The ultimate fun, we think, and some will escape unscathed, but not many. This is the end of the twentieth century. They will not tell us that men and women are the same in our adolescence because too much money can be made off the difference. No mothers are they who wax fat by mining the rich fields of adolescent passion. Masquerading as "artist," using the most sophisticated tools of communication known to man, they will dick and pussy you to death. Lead you, in your vulnerable and unsophisticated state, down the road of romantic indigestion. Give you in too-large doses what you have already.

This is no vaccination, it is an infection. Imposed on the young by their elders for profit at the expense of music, film, dance, and literature. And you love it. Like the many Africans given umbrellas, beads, and mirrors in exchange for humans. The joyful trading of something priceless for trinkets. We accept mass-media images of our young romances—no, sexuality, we are now too hip for romance. And as we languish toward adulthood, our feelings being ripened too quickly, they who have raped our future will go on to lay new frontiers to waste. Like the many who thoroughly plundered the less sophisticated inhabitants of the New World for centuries.

But this is still only just the end of the twentieth century. On the long time line of the so-human search for a profound and lasting happiness, many of us will still have our romances. Of the senses and the mind. We will have our spring dances, our candlelight dinners, our Valentine's Days, our ear when we need to talk, our moonlit hand-holdings, our horizon gazings, our car rides in sensual silence. We will come in out of the cold lone-

liness of our individuality. Out-In, Out-In, 2/4 time medium tempo, swinging. In 3/4 time waltzing, no, shuffling in 6/8, a combination of both. We are ready to understand how things are or can be between us. We can rise above even romancing the mind of another to a higher, calmer place. We accept love graciously, without reservation, greedily, quickly, slowly, for life depends on it. Civilized life. A style imposed on the basics, like the blues.

We are men and women in love with each other's maleness and femaleness. No longer under the intoxicating influence of hormones and fads, the intensity of our interactions comes from intimate knowledge of each other and a willingness to learn more. No authority to rebel against. No mother's love to part with, no peer group to satisfy. We are ourselves free to affirm God's great gift, life of the senses.

Perhaps these same senses are also participants in a cruel trick to obfuscate our hunger for the divine. Keep us satisfied with a good meal, a songbird, a sensual touch, a stimulating conversation, and we'll never rise above the titillating to the beyond-the-senses calm of heaven. Perhaps, but these senses are our birthright. God offers pleasure as divine revelation, the devil proffers it to deceive. But God does offer pleasure.

When they tell you that romance is a projection of the imagination, scoff at such silliness. Romance is an intense relationship with reality. If you are lucky or optimistic, it is always beautiful or becoming beautiful. If you are pessimistic or unlucky, you have a bad time.

You will hear that men and women are the same, and publicly you will agree, except on holidays and in moonlit rooms around the world. At these times you will be reacquainted with your oldest selves. Playing with a fire that has burned even before the arrival of Prometheus. Playing like Adam and Eve in the garden, willing victims of the serpent, standing naked and ashamed and embarrassed, but happy. Yes, happy at being given the choice to participate in their own fate. The chance to romance each other and the world, or fail.

They will tell you, tell you, and tell you, but you are now like the jazzmen who stomp, hop, jump, slap, shout, cry, laugh, eat, and cuss the blues with accuracy and feeling. Experience and a willingness to participate have qualified you to play the game without the stifling hand of guilt covering your mouth.

Just as these jazzmen bend the possibilities of sound with abandon and joy, a sensuousness possessed by only the most confident, so do you fearlessly bend the heartstrings of the world. You love this participation, you love the learning—discovery, recognition, understanding, acceptance, in 6/8 time they equal love itself. You make love to the world because you know the attempt will always be accepted. Not just by her who was once your sole source of inspiration, but now by the Creator of this playground that you have been bequeathed with but one command, "Love." That is romance. Willful participation with style and in the groove, like the many jazzmen who have swung their way across this globe throughout the twentieth century.

Armed with a willingness to make the many who came to participate happy, they swing the blues away by playing the blues. By playing willingly with the most intimate, intense facts of life.

You will hear that pain produces beauty. Do not believe this foolishness. Joy in spite of pain, to spite pain, that is the substance of beauty. We are forgiven honest failures in search of romance. Feel no guilt. It is our duty to seek a kindness, a lovingness, a sweetness. We are men and women at our best when we romance all of each other and the world.

Let us not forget the colors of nature expressed in patterns on clothing—the changing moods of the earth as the sun and moon pass proudly through the sky. The beauty of seasons and dawns, dusks, and midnights. Let us not forget the sweetness of so many whispers from the gurgling coos of park streams to the slow hum of a late-night automobile. From the throbbing stillness of interlocked lovers to the sensual textures of words and music organized to inspire and satiate. Let us not forget to chew slowly as we savor our most loved meal. Eat not only with respect for the skill of whoever has prepared this fine repast, but also to dignify the surrendering of life so that we may continue in style. One day we, too, will be on the plate. Let us remember to savor the warm coolness of another's mouth and tongue and lips softly but deliberately locked and unlocked. In-Out, In-Out, in 3/4, no 2/4, no 6/8 time playing. Enjoy it. Playing the blues away with kindness. Remember the fragrance of many fields of flowers or department stores or soulful homes or the pungence of our most intimate interactions.

Do not feel guilty. Enjoy what we have been given. As the schoolkids used to say, "If you don't use it, you lose it." Let us not forget the range of textures and shapes and touch, like a blind man slowly proceeding sequentially to learn the meaning of each shape. Then remembering. Remembering the ins and outs of every environment by feel. Remembering to touch greedily, desperately, hungrily, slowly, patiently, happily, then thoroughly in a ritual we have enjoyed since before fire. Hell, this *was* fire. It is still. Capable of warming the coldest regions. Capable of singeing, burning, destroying. It's like the blues, not to be played with but played. With accuracy, skill, concentration, with a lovingness, a sweetness, a kindness. With soul, yes, with soul.

Let us not forget the mind. Learning continues, unrestricted by age or sex or health or to the bedroom. All that is required is a willingness to participate. And we love it. We can return at will to any point of our lives and be that, at least temporarily. We can use all of our insights as they come. All at once or slowly. We can advance into worlds of feeling never before known, and play.

This choice is the beauty of adulthood, of knowledge, of human life: we can gather as much of life as we can fathom up into ourselves and make love to it. And what we can't fathom, we can learn about or create. Without fear, without guilt, we plunge into the chaos of existence armed only with a willingness to swing. And with that we romance the world. As for me, I'll settle for a simple phone number, please.

They will tell you that this is the end of the twentieth century, and all is lost.

Any jazzman can tell you that "they" are like the blues. Just ask Mr. Murray. No one can identify "them." But "they" exist, and love to play the game. "They" love to destroy a groove. "They" have to be swung, or "they"'ll swing you. Any jazzman can tell you, "Swinging is our business, accept life in 6/8 time." March or waltz—no, both, shuffle. No guilt. Keep moving and learning and acting on knowledge. Enjoy it, bask in it, play in it with soul and feeling. Once again, with feeling. The world is our birthright. Love it. In-Out, In-Out, In- . . . that final out and the game, the romance, is over.

Now we are above thought and feeling. Gone on to greater experiences. But we have been prepared by the world in the same fashion that our many mothers nourished our first stages of development. With lovingkindness, sometimes sternly. We are not afraid. We stand naked of our bodies with this knowledge. Romance is an intense relationship with reality. If you are lucky and optimistic, it is always beautiful or becoming beautiful. If you are unlucky or pessimistic, you have a bad-ass time. In our final romance with the creator of all we offer no excuses, only ourselves. We are, of course, accepted and loved. In all keys, time signatures, and doing all steps, we say to ourselves, yes, yes, yass.

They will tell you that men and women are the same. Not on holidays, though, or in moonlit bedrooms. At least not yet. This is the end of the twentieth century, we still love our maleness and femaleness. We still love our twilight dinners, low tv glows, morning sunshines, dancing dates, sentimental songs, silent smiles, eye winks, hand-holdings, phone exchanges, awkward revelations, standoffish flirtations, disappointments. Yes, disappointments. They let us know that we are playing the game. That we are mortally locked in the sweet embrace of life. Outside of whose clutches lies—more of the same. That is the kindest twist of all, we don't really have that much of a choice. Pain is in the world. But have you ever tried to kill a fly? He doesn't just fly away, he flies his ass off.

7. BREAK

You could be on the "Wyoming Hereford Ranch," about to put the best meat you will ever taste into your mouth. If you are invited by Anna Marie and Sloan Hales, and if you know how to act, as they say in the country. That means: Yes, sir, or ma'am, thank you, please; good morning, afternoon, evening, and night; saying grace and smiling graciously. Someone could suggest that you engage in the world's oldest athletic contest. You could race under that big open Wyoming sky, beneath the gaze of those majestic mountains, and lose, but not ungraciously. Grace will be said at the table, after all.

YOU COULD BE IN MORNINGTIME NEW ORLEANS, sun pouring through a window in Miss Dolores' kitchen. Jason scans the *TV Guide*'s baseball schedule. Delfeayo cracks a joke in his Lonjalfian style, Mboya keeps his eye on Mr. Ellis. Mboya is autistic. He never talks, only sighs through his nose like a miniature steam engine. He jumps up and organizes anything out of place in a room. But maybe he avoids looking at the table now, so he won't have to rearrange the jars of syrup and preserves that are out of order. You almost never know what he is thinking, except in this instance his thoughts will soon become ours.

How will we graciously eat the biscuits that our daddy is so proudly making? Is there enough syrup to drown the taste? Perhaps Miss Dolores will step in and rescue our morning. Well, okay, at least we will be able to wash them down with her good New Orleans chicory coffee. But Mboya, he

doesn't drink coffee. He also doesn't have to say thank you. Waffles and biscuits and pancakes, things that require syrup, always seem like dessert to me anyway. Give me grits, eggs, and I'm sorry, some bacon. Please.

OR YOU COULD BE PRESENT on the birthday of our interim pianist, Stephen Scott. We each take turns saluting him with our best wishes for his future health and success. Then we break out the champagne and a gift. We do this for every birthday, accomplishment, arrival, or departure of our members. Everyone salutes in his unique style. Homey is always soulful, Veal is always brief and direct, Rob is always insightful. It takes at least thirty minutes, is done after a gig, and feels good.

IF YOU KNOW HOW TO ACT, you could be invited to a post-tour dinner by the great Argentinian impresario Alejandro Sterenfeld. After playing a concert in the Palacio des Bella Artes in Mexico City, you go to a fine restaurant and feast on the great stories Maestro Sterenfeld has amassed in his forty-odd years of concert promotion. He is a man of great dignity, integrity, and style. If you know how to act, he can teach you many things about how to live. It's never just another concert to him or just another day. At the end of the evening we toast the maestro with our bottles of Sidral Mundet.

YOU COULD BE THE recipient of an extreme act of generosity and soul in Winston-Salem, North Carolina, at the home of Diane Caesar. Perhaps you complained about the hour-long drive after the gig, but when that first barbecued chicken wing touched your mouth . . .

You later joined the rest of the brothers combing through garbage cans to see if any meat was left on discarded bones. Some of us sucked the marrow. After one of the finest meals ever prepared, the most educated road manager in the world, Lolis Elie, also known as the Reverend Possessor, the owner of three degrees in the literary arts from reputable universities, will summon his gargantuan skills as an improvising verbalizer to put all of our thank yous into one extended and humorous sermon in the style of the Right Honorable Reverend Cleroy Zebedee Eldridge III of the Holiness Baptist Church.

"I have been requested to speak. I will do so, but not for long. What I have to say will be brief, but potent. Just as potent as the gases that escape our bodies as we digest this fine meal.

"Tonight we have been returned to a tradition thought lost to the ages. ["Yes."] For we have all heard tell of Dionysian feasts. ["Yes, we have."] And we know that Odysseus, the storm-tossed wanderer, said that people announced themselves as civilized or barbarian by the way they treated travelers. ["Mm-humm."] Moreover, Odysseus opined that the degree of their civilization was marked by the degree of their hospitality. ["Yes, he did."] Now this was not new. ["No, it wasn't."] This wisdom was ancient before Odysseus. ["Come on, now."] It sprang up with humanity itself, and it has been tested many times and across times, from Cairo, Egypt, to Cairo, Illinois. ["You tellin' it." "Go 'head."] Tonight we have landed on a shore where civilization not only exists but flourishes. ["You gettin' warm, now."] Tonight we find ourselves at a welcome table where Odysseus himself, where all the ancient kings and queens, would recognize the royalty of our hostess and unhesitatingly pledge their fellowship. ["Okay, okay." "Tell it."]

"I was speaking of Odysseus, a Greek, and we cannot pass on from this Greek without remembering that he gave lessons in gratitude as well as hospitality. ["He did, he did."] Lest we be like those suitors to Penelope, who squandered and disrespected Odysseus's substance in his absence, and paid for it with their arrogant lives on his return ["Have mercy." "Oh, no." "Lawd, Lawd."], we offer thanks for this meal not out of fear but with all humility. ["There it is." "He said it." "Go on, Rev'und."] Tonight we have enjoyed a repast of such homespun grandeur, so soulfully and intelligently prepared, that we are almost moved to tears. Tears of extreme joy. ["Ha-ha-ha."] When next we go hungry on the road, as we know we will ["Yes."], in a cold night on a distant shore ["Yes."], we will reflect upon this evening's warmth and love. ["Yessuh."] We will speak of Diane, and we will say that if anything should be preserved from American culture, it must be she. ["Must be."]

"Now many will say, what does this have to do with crack, teenage pregnancy, black-on-black crime, apathy in the community? I must tell you, everything. Because the way to combat disillusionment is with achievement. And achievement's crowning glory is greatness. That is Diane. ["Say that." "She is." "Diane." "Alright." "You the Reverend tonight."] She is in line with our most magnificent ancestors, her name should be etched in the culinary history of the American Negro. Thank you. God bless you. Amen.

"The collection will be taken shortly."

OR YOU COULD BE IN CHIBA, JAPAN. In a small club called Elvin for the great drummer Elvin Jones. If you are lucky, you could play this small club with Elvin himself, and after the gig Keiko Jones, Elvin's wife, would fix a fine Japanese meal with all types of cooked and uncooked fish, plenty of sake, and fried tofu. In this soulful club where local people come to have

a good time, you would recall Miss Mary's bar in Hanson City, Louisiana, next door to where you lived as a boy for a short time. Then if you sat down to the piano and started to play a shuffle, Reginald Veal would show the locals how to second-line around our table. But if you were a little boy and it was two A.M., you would probably just fall asleep and miss it all!

YOU COULD BE IN ROCHESTER, NEW YORK, and have the opportunity to see the great dancers of Garth Fagan Dance. Sit right in on a rehearsal and even write some music for them. And if you have your horn, play something to accompany choreography as intimate as any that you or anyone else will ever see. Then, if you sound good enough, be asked to play an impromptu piece to celebrate the collaboration. Good-time time.

OR IF YOU KNOW the one and only Toon-Yab Scob, Sugar Sweet Rob, you might get invited to an after-gig party in St. Louis, an old-fashioned house party where you can shake your behind in 4/4 time. All night long.

YOU COULD BE IN MARCIAC, FRANCE, invited to an estate for a daytime paté party. Have the opportunity to profile as if the estate is yours, eat some of the richest foie gras in the world, drink some of the finest wine, then play the blues with Warm Daddy and Cone for the entertainment of all. And, if

you are especially friendly, you will be asked by a particularly endearing lady to play one more for her. You play "Stardust," and she breaks down into tears. "That song reminds me of the American soldiers during World War II. I'm sorry, it's just . . . Thank you, thank you." As you survey the grape fields in traditional garb, as you converse about the history of the estate, as you joke with the wine makers, you think about this woman. Yes, ma'am. Thank you.

THEN IN THE EVENING you could be invited into an extremely soulful home for a meal *à la bonne français,* as they say.

YOU COULD BE IN A hot gym in Philadelphia, deeply involved in a totally insignificant basketball game that is the central focus of your world. Your elbow is out too far to the left, so you probably missed that shot, but that won't affect the incessant pre- and postgame bragging. Win or lose, it's how you talk the game that counts. Then you go get a cheese steak.

OR YOU COULD BE the recipient of a trumpet from the excellent trumpeter Demo Morselli in Milan, Italy. And be told by his exquisitely beautiful wife, Lucia, that Demo loves "Lucia, *la tromba, e* Wynton." Then you could hear Demo unleash his swing and humor through the horn, and feel fortunate to be a trumpeter. And then enjoy a big Italian meal.

MAYBE YOU STOPPED through Chicago. The greatest trumpet maker in the world, Dave Monette, is there. If you play trumpet, you are in heaven. You try one horn that is freshly made while he adjusts the other. He loves to hear good jazz music and eat Indian food. When he shows up to our concerts, and he might show up anywhere at anytime, he says, "I've come to purify my ears." I call him Doctor, he calls me Professor. He loves to hear

his horns sing and swing. He says, "Play 'Embraceable You' for me. Let me hear how the horn sounds." Then he says, "It's the player, man. The player."

Once, when I was rehearsing for a recording in Providence, Rhode Island, with pianist Judy Stillman, I dropped a slide and completely destroyed the sound of the instrument. We were recording on Monday, and this was the Saturday morning before. Monette flew from Chicago to Providence that night and fixed the horn. Judy and I played the Hindemith Sonata so he could hear if the adjustments worked. Just the three of us in a small recital hall at Brown University. I played as much horn as I have ever played, showing thanks to the Doctor. When we finished, he had to catch a plane back to Chicago to teach a yoga class on Sunday morning. I asked him, "How much do I owe you, Doc?" He said, "Man, you sure played the shit out of that Hindemith." Thank you, Doctor Monette.

OR YOU COULD FIND YOURSELF in St. Giles' Church in London with the English Chamber Orchestra. As you stand across from a statue of Sir Thomas Busby, you play the Haydn Trumpet Concerto under the baton of Maestro Raymond Leppard, a first-class musician, conductor, and thinker. If you are polite, you will have many interesting conversations with orchestra members on subjects from the Holocaust to scones. If you know how to act, they will play with gusto even though this may be their third session of the day. If you play well, they'll love you because there won't be too many takes.

And Raymond, he can't make Wednesday night's session because he has a dinner engagement with the queen, but when he returns, the tempos will still be the same. He has the most impeccable sense of time. I recorded the same music—Haydn, Hummel, Mozart—ten years ago and decided to do it again just to make sure I haven't been wasting time. I love playing with this orchestra. They liked the vest.

OR YOU COULD BE ON VACATION, but . . . it wouldn't be as much fun. That's why I never take one.

8 BRIDGE

"Bags at five, leave at six." That's A.M., as in no-man's-land for the jazz musician. You went to sleep at 4:30, and now the bellman is knocking on the door. Your head barely had time to dent the pillow. "Hey, man, can you come back and get me in ten minutes?"

"That's what the last two gentlemen said, sir. I have to get these bags."

"Shit! Okay, okay." Out of bed to the door with two bags weighed down by interrupted slumber, drawers and socks hanging out the sides.

"Thank you, sir."

"Yeah, man. Thank you." Wash face, brush teeth, the whole elementary school morning routine, then look out the window to see something, anything. Many times you can see whole sections of a city, and you are always surprised at how many JESUS SAVES lighted crosses dot the landscape. Cities feel different in the morning, fresher, unused, optimistic. They wake up differently, just like people. Some creep up, some jump up. But if I had a choice, I would only see cities go to sleep.

On this Florida morning a sweet fog thickens the sky, and on the horizon a hesitant sun reflects this sweetness over and through the trees like the web of a giant golden spider, sticky and inescapable. You surrender to it. Downstairs beneath the flags, the bus of Harold Russell patiently waits to chew up America's roads, carrying a cargo of Negroes intent upon freely swinging the blues away. In Florida, no less, some two hundred and fifty years after the same cargo would have been swinging against the incessant

bite of an overseer's lash. It is time to don your bus garb and proceed with haste to your bunk. Maybe you can grab a little sleep, but probably you will converse or argue with the cats, miss the sleep, and go through the rest of the day's activities fatigued.

Then there is morning bus call in Pennsylvania. Amidst the mountains the air sparkles, clear and brisk, it feels like your mouth after a strong peppermint. Stand in that November air for five minutes, and you are awake for the rest of the week. This particular day is special because of the presence of Mr. Albert Murray. Mr. Murray knows a little bit about everything and a lot about a lot. He loves knowledge, swing, and excellence. Whenever we see him we feel good, 'cause swing is in the house. Extension, elaboration, and refinement, that's Mr. Murray's definition of the artistic process. If you talk to him for two seconds, you'll learn something useful. He can cook some chitlins, too.

I was introduced to Mr. Murray by Stanley Crouch. Crouch is a writer and intellectual of the first magnitude. He developed my hunger to understand the arts. He reminds me of men in the barbershop when I was growing up, except that he is infinitely more accurate in his assessments. He has tremendous integrity and courage. It was surprising to meet someone with such intellectual acumen who wasn't corny, and who would hang his foot into somebody's ass if provoked. I talk to Crouch almost every day. I'll be forever grateful for all the stuff he has taught me.

Crouch loves him some Al. When I first met Crouch, in 1980, all he would talk about was Al, Al. After he took me to Mr. Murray's house, I could see why. First, Mr. Murray has 10 million books and can pull from the shelves at will with exact page numbers to support his angle on any discussion. It could be the Civil War, William Faulkner, mythology, physics, you name it. For the first three or four years of being around Crouch and him, I just nodded my head and added a foggy "Mm-hmm" to conversations on issues I didn't know anything about. That was most of the time.

Mr. Murray wrote the book on the blues, *Stomping the Blues.* Being around Mr. Murray teaches you what fifty years of sustained engagement with American culture yields. He is one of the very greatest men in the United States, and in everything I do I want to make him proud. His wife, Mozelle, fixes the best fruitcake in New York City, and if you're ever on 132nd Street maybe you can get some, too. I put my hat on this morning out of respect to Mr. Murray. Before we leave, he tells me, "Keep swinging." I can tell that he is proud.

HAROLD RUSSELL is the Paganini of bus. He knows the road, he knows and loves his bus. He always arrives exactly on time. He drives with authority in every kind of weather through every terrain. He carries the map of America in his head. He's driven 3 million miles without a single accident. He can get lit up, too, but only on his day off.

He's a pure Southerner. His first words in the morning, "Do I have all of my men? Hey, Reggie [as in Veal], what's happening? Let's get airborne." His wife, Darlene, comes out to ride the bus every now and then. If she can't, she sends us some of her good banana bread. Miss Darlene's bread never makes it past the city limits. We all love Harold and Darlene.

Harold's got to have his cigarettes and his black coffee. You could see Harold being a cowboy in the Old West. He's a workman, tough, with a hearty constitution, he can stay up all night and talk plenty of shit. Harold's people used to work on the land. He sometimes speaks of how they got up in the morning and had to hit it, that whole farming situation back in Tennessee. Harold is soulful, yeah, Harold has a lot of soul. He'll tell you about hunting possum, and how they cooked that greasy possum. I asked him if he liked possum, he said hell, no, but he liked the way they cooked it. I told him frog, possum, squirrel, all taste like chicken to me. He said, "Sheeet!" drawing the word out like a drag on one of his Marlboros.

Harold is country. I'm country, so is Veal, and Wycliffe. Wes is country, too, even though he's from Brooklyn. I grew up in Kenner, Louisiana, that's sure enough country. I like the country and country people. In little towns like Kenner you see the drainage ditches dug beside the side of the road (especially in the black section), dogs running around loose, sweet shop on the corner one block from the barroom/pool hall/dance floor, houses with tin roofs and red sparkly tile sides. Harold Russell knows about that. He can get mad, too. We call him the pit bull. Little but tenacious. He'll get hotter than hell if messed with. Or, in his words, "hotter'n a fresh fucked fox in a forest fire." Harold's something, man.

SOMETIMES WE WATCH VIDEOS on the bus to pass the time. Wes is our designated programmer. He chooses the proper video for the occasion and operates all machinery. In that role Warm Daddy becomes Captain Video. His tastes range from the ecclesiastic to the tawdry. That's why he's the captain. There are front-room and back-room videos. In the front room we generally watch tapes of jazz musicians, movies, and nature videos. We'll constantly stop tapes to discuss what we are seeing.

"Look at how small the neck is on Paul Chambers' bass."

"Roll that back and check out the expression on Lady Day's face, man. Damn! What you think she was thinking about then?"

"Man, I think she was in love with Pres, I think they had a thing."

"Naw, man, you crazy."

"Look at how Trane is standing. I'm telling you, that's some tech*nique.*"

"What you think was going through Trane's head when he was playing all of that bad shit?"

"Man, I don't know. But I'm gonna tell you what, it don't look like Elvin liked what Dolphy was dealing with. Roll it back and look at that look he gave him. Roll it. Yeah.

Right there! Freeze it, man, look at that. Man, that's some grit Elvin threw on Dolphy."

There's one Duke Ellington tape we rewound eighty times, where Paul Gonsalves gets up to solo and is so inebriated, he heads away from the mike.

In the front room you also hear, "Man, if they offered you that money, would you take it?" "The villain is gonna try to kill her now." "Man, where do they get the money to make these sad movies?" In the lounge in the back of the bus you hear no conversation, only exclamations.

Eric Reed is another champion of video and the almanac of a thousand and one unbelievable facts. Famous people who died on their sixty-fourth birthday. What Brando really said in the fifth scene of *The Godfa-*

ther. He must watch *The Godfather* once a week. He and Wycliffe and Veal also like to watch gospel revues.

Traveling the road is an endless series of "Are we here?" The worst of which is a truck stop or greasy spoon when you think it's gonna be the hotel. The mornings are also difficult because the toilet sometimes doesn't work, especially if someone (who, we never know) forgets the golden rule: no sitting on the potty. The landscape of America is increasingly dotted with prefabricated malls and fast-food joints, but we are fortunate to have Harold Russell, who knows where the hip, slightly out-of-the-way cafeterias are.

WE ENJOY many a good hot argument on the bus, in cars, or even in airports. Many times it will start over a newspaper article.

"You see this article comparing rock stars to Bach and Beethoven?"

"Where?"

"Right here, man."

"Let me see that. Damn, sure is."

"Man, they talking about Bach and Beethoven and them from Gretna, Louisiana, not the Germans."

"Oh."

"Now they saying that Clinton has a chance against Bush."

"I don't think so."

"Man, I bet those two young white boys are going to stomp on Bush and them."

"I don't know, man. You know Bush represents good old traditional American values: Let's keep our foot up a nigger's ass."

"Yeah, and call it something else, like redistribution."

"Man, at the rate we are going, our own foot is so far up our behinds, ain't no room for Bush's."

"Wait a second, man. Let's seriously examine Bush's policies." That's Lolis. He will tilt every conversation toward political facts. "Bush

vetoed the extension of the Civil Rights Act, the original of which his predecessor, Reagan, lobbied against in 1964. He claimed to veto it because it contained quotas."

"Hold on, man." That's me. I tilt everything toward art. "He vetoed it because that's what he thinks his people want. His people means those who elected him, and that includes very few Negroes. He's like a musician who constantly chases trends. He's always behind, trying to be popular by imitating stereotyped behavior. Afraid to act on his own vision."

"Man, are you going to sit here and pretend that George Bush's 'vision' of America is something that includes civil rights?"

Rob will philosophize, he'll bring in Malraux or Thomas Mann. Rob can get fired up in a verbal exchange, cussin' and hollering. Not Lolis, he's like a hired assassin. He stays calm and rational—and polite. Rob is like me. We stick to our point—especially when we are wrong. Then admit it much later, sometimes.

"In *The Coming Victory of Democracy* Thomas Mann says that democracy is a superior form of governing because it is based on recognizing the dignity of man. The Dignity of Man, gotdammit. Not white man or black man, but man, which includes *wo*man. Do you think Bush's vision has respect for the dignity of Negroes, women, or poor white folks for that matter? Man, you know better than that!"

One of our most memorable discussions was on the Clarence Thomas affair. Opinion was divided, as usual.

"Man, did you see those hearings? Boy, America is a trip. Race relations is a trip."

"I think she was telling the truth."

"The truth about what, that he asked her for some pussy two times?"

"I think those investigators sold her out. Her privacy should have been protected."

"Yeah, that's true, but it is funny. Clarence Thomas, black as night, but always supporting policies that work against the interest of black folks. Country-assed, Georgian, Uncle Tom Negro, with a lily-white wife sitting by in full support, even crying for his black, long-pipe-having ass, while a group of secretary-harassing, twenty- and thirty-year pussy-hunting, corrupt-ass cracker senators try to protect his ability to serve this country honorably against the testimony of big round boodied Anita Hill, who probably reminds them of all the black pussy they've had or bought or wanted. And—this is really the trip—the only reason he's up for nomination to our highest court in the first place is because he's thoroughly unqualified."

"Whew, boy. Life is a bitch."

"Yeah, ole Jefferson Davis would turn over in his Confederate-ass grave."

"Not because of the nomination, though. Because of his wife."

"Look, man, this is not a joke. That could be your momma or sister or daughter having to go to work every day with a boss who's constantly aggravating her. Or it could be you."

"Sheet. I'm not that lucky."

"I'm talking about a man."

"Man, come on."

"No, man, I'm serious. Sexual harassment is some serious shit."

"Man, look, you know she gave Thomas some pussy and got mad when he married that white woman."

"She ain't as mad as those white-ass senators."

"I bet Kennedy ain't mad."

"But what's really a trip is how many people want to watch this insipid, tawdry bullshit."

"You want to watch it. Don't lie. And you lovin' it."

"I wish they had me up there—'Did you try to have relations with this woman?' 'Not tried, sir, did. And it was good. Damned good!' "

"Man, y'all ain't ready. Y'all ain't ready at all. This is not funny."

Then Lolis says, "Let's examine Clarence Thomas' record in 198—"

"Wait a second. Yesterday, you said it wasn't about Clarence Thomas, but now—"

"I changed my mind, which is something that would benefit you from time to time."

A LIMOUSINE IS a big car with drinks in the back. The television never works, but you don't have to worry about opening the door. Of course, since

you've been opening car doors for yourself as long as you can remember, waiting to have the door opened takes longer than the ride. Limousine drivers generally know a great deal about where the happenings are, however, and they always have great stories to tell.

When we reach the airport there's either no time or way too much. When we've got three hours to wait, we'll get some airport food (have mercy), look in the shops (which are triply overpriced), read, or sleep. We'll flirt with the passersby, that's the best way to pass time. It always begins, "Where are you or y'all from?" Then who knows. Plane routes are like roads in the United States. You always have the feeling that you can get anywhere from anywhere. You are truly *in the world*.

"Are you all some kind of team or something?"

"Sorry, sir, we oversold this plane. What is your name again?"

"Can you open this bag, please?"

Here's Rob. "Look, this is obscene and absurd. Surely you are not going to charge as much overweight as we have paid for our tickets."

"Those are our rules, Mr. Robinson."

"I am not against paying a reasonable amount for this."

"What do you think this is, *Let's Make a Deal?*"

"Give me my luggage! I'll get another airline." Then along comes a supervisor, and the amount gets reduced by more than a third.

Once I convinced a customs officer to board the plane before takeoff and pretend to have found something illegal in one of our bags. Another time Cone and I played "King Porter Stomp" in the Rio de Janeiro airport. More than once, we've missed connections and had to ponder our dilemmas in buses, cars, planes, sometimes walking. Many times it is a pain, and then someone will say, "Did you see what they wrote about those riots in Copenhagen after the split vote on the Maastricht treaty?"

"The what?"

"On the unification of Europe."

"The unification of Europe? Never happen."

"That's what they said about Germany. Man, you never know what's going to happen out here."

"Come on, man, let's go. We got a plane to catch."

9. VAMP

Vamping establishes a point of reference. Something needs to be repeated, and is. You can vamp any part of a tune. In front, a vamp creates an atmosphere. In the middle, it provides a familiar place to rest. At the end, it's something comfortable you can tap your foot to on the way out.

The blues has a twelve-bar form.

To improvise means attempting to improve by working with whatever is available.

Swing is a matter of ongoing coordination and participation.

The ultimate achievement in jazz soloing is the expression of a distinctive personality.

The ultimate achievement in jazz music is the interplay of distinctive personalities through some type of musical form. The group establishes its identity with this interplay while swinging.

Jazz is musical interplay on blues-based melodies, harmonies, rhythms, and textures in the motion of an improvised groove. A groove is the successful coordination of differing parts—like a clock.

"What is your name again?" a little kid asks.

"Wynton. W, y, n, t, o, n."

"Can you play 'Sesame Street'?" "How loud can you play?"

"WAAAMP!"

"Oowee!" "Ouch!" "Hee-hee-hee!"

"How long have you been playing?"

"Twenty-five years."

"Wow, man, you old."

"What?"

"Do you know Michael Jackson?"

"No."

"Can you teach me how to play?"

"Come up here. Now buzz your lips like this. Um-humm. Keep doing it. Now do it into the horn."

"Braamp!"

"You are a natural trumpeter."

"Can you get us out of school for the rest of the day?"

"If you answer all of my questions correctly, I will. How many bars in the blues form?"

"I don't know." "Twelve!" "Stop that!"

"What does improvise mean?"

"To improve." "Make up something." "Huh?"

"What is swinging?"

"In the park." "Give me that." "Hee-hee-hee." "Being together."

"Very, very good. Now, if you answer this last one right, no more school for the whole day. In what year did Louis Armstrong record 'West End Blues'?"

"Aw, man." "To improve!" "No fair." "Who?" "Being together." "1985." "Twelve bars!"

"Well, sorry, back to class. But thank you very much."

"Thank you, Mr. Marsalis." Then the children present me with the school cap or a T-shirt, which I proudly wear, and if we are lucky we play a little basketball in the gym. The principal shows us out.

"Thank you for coming. The children will remember this."

"Well, maybe they won't remember the blues form or my name, but I hope they remember I got them out of math for one day."

PEOPLE ARE EATING all of the fruit in our dressing room. One boy's parents and friends are nervous, but happy. He asks, "How do I develop my sound?" This is the best question to ask, because the sound is the foundation of playing.

"Take a deep breath, like a yawn. Relax. Do long tones from middle G to low F-sharp every morning. But soft, like a whisper; just sit still and concentrate on controlling the flow of the air, opening the sound while playing softly, filling the entire horn, projecting your best personality through the horn, and looking good. I'm serious. If you look good, you probably will sound good. I mean with your embouchure and what not. Here, take my horn and try it. Soft, now, very soft." He has a big, pretty, warm sound.

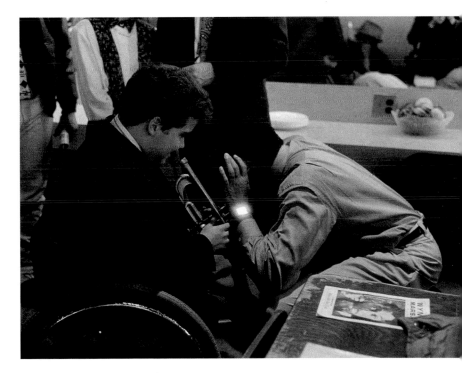

"DON'T PLAY WITH the rim of the mouthpiece on the red of your lips. The muscle goes around your lips, so when you place the mouthpiece below the muscle your endurance suffers. Try this new embouchure. Okay, wait, let me hold it up so you can see how it should feel. Now I know this is difficult, but I really think you should change to this. Practice every day in a mirror and make sure your embouchure looks like this. Mm-hmm."

"Are you sure that I should change?"

"Well, it's ultimately up to you, but I think you should. Get a Max Schlossberg *Daily Drills* book and practice the first three pages slowly. Good luck."

"Thank you, Mr. Marsalis, thank you."

"Wynton, please, just Wynton. You gonna be alright, just make sure you practice every day."

"TO IMPROVISE MEANS TO IMPROVE. To improve a thing, you must first know what it is. You can't do algebra if you can't add. You can't improvise if you don't know the melody or can't hear the chord progression. Painful

but true. But it's also true that since everyone knows something, anyone can begin to improvise. Just find one note and play with the rhythm. Yeah, that's it.

"If you're telling a story, you don't say, 'I went to the store and came home.' You say, 'You will never believe what happened to me on the way to the store.' Make your phrases interesting by injecting your personality. That's it, don't be shy, it's always hard at first. Keep trying. You don't have to be a virtuoso; just find what you can play and play with that.

"Learn to hear melodies, you don't have time to think about chords when you play. Practice hearing the chord progression at home. Start with the bass notes. If you can hear the bass line, you can figure out the harmonies. Remember to develop your personality: play your way—but still learn the changes. You have more fun when you know what is going on.

"Don't slouch when you play. You too young to be slouching. Face the audience. Once you start playing, it's too late to hide.

"Swing is like dancing. Swing is a group of musicians dancing notes and rhythms with style through a form. This is a complex song that you are playing, but y'all sound good. Let me show you how to play the changes."

Some of these kids drove over a hundred miles to attend the clinic, then I sat down and played the wrong progression. In front of their band director. "Let's try that again. Oh! Okay."

ONE FRIDAY AFTERNOON at six P.M., Wes and I visit Ron Carter's band at Lincoln High School in East St. Louis. He has a great band every year. I first visited his school in 1980 and try to return whenever we stop through St. Louis. In general, high school and college bands sound good playing arrangements, but when the improvising starts, the swinging ends. But Ron Carter puts his kids on a vibe. He always has four or five excellent soloists. And they're well disciplined.

"How do you tongue when playing bebop?" one student asks.

"Sing it, then try to imitate what you have sung on your instrument."

"How do you keep your place in the form?" asks another.

"Learn to hear the harmonic progression. Learn to use the devices of jazz. Let us show you. Wes'll play the piano, I'll play the drums. This is call and response . . . this is a riff . . . this is interwoven improvisation . . . this is how to develop a theme.

"Whenever you solo, try to develop your themes by interacting with the other musicians' themes. Let's play together and listen to how Wes and I support the soloist and maintain a musical dialogue. Everybody should take a couple of choruses. . . . Yes." After twenty minutes we started swinging so hard, Mr. Carter had to pull out his horn and clarify a thing or two. He loves to swing, and that's why his band always does, too! Wes tells the kids to get in the woodshed and practice. "Shed and shed alike," he says. That's something to vamp on.

"WHAT DO YOU THINK about rap music?"

"Rappers have interesting haircuts."

"But they're talking about what's happening today."

"Yeah, like what?"

"Racism and stuff."

"What solutions do they give you for that?"

"That it's wrong."

"That's a solution?"

"What solution does jazz give?"

"First, it teaches you to think across a longer than twenty-five-second form. Second, it teaches you how to communicate with others. Third, it makes you develop your personality through practice and contemplation. Fourth, it puts you into contact with some of the greatest musical minds of the twentieth century. Fifth, your ears don't ring after a gig. Sixth, you don't have to keep reaching for your pipe in public."

"What does that have to do with life in the city?"

"Where are you from?"

"The street."

"You mean you live on the street?"

"No, but I know what's happening in the street."

"If you know that, you know it's something to avoid."

"Man, you ain't hip."

"Hip to what? That corny slang, all that cussin', posturing, and whining, calling girls bitches, that monotonous beat, antisocial behavior, and a philosophy that doesn't include anyone who doesn't think and act like you?"

"Man, you the one excluding anyone who don't think like you."

"I'm including you."

"Not all rap is about that bad stuff."

"The kind you like is. Look at how you're dressed."

"Rappers is serious about what they doing."

"So are Republicans."

"Well, that's what I like."

"I liked the blaxploitation movies I grew up with, and the platform shoes and the bell-bottom pants and the pimps."

"So what? You have your opinion, I got mine. This is America, I don't have to think like you."

"Most rappers say America ain't shit."

"It ain't."

"Well, you American, you may have a point."

"Man, it's easy for you to stand up there and talk. You probably not even from the 'hood. You don't know about what's happening out here."

"Since when did someone have to be from your neighborhood to teach you something? Most of what you will learn, if you are interested in learning anything, comes from places and people much more different from you than me."

"Rappers are communicating with the people."

"Son, communication is an activity. *That* they are communicating is not the issue. The question is, *what* are they communicating? Communication is like a pipeline. What are you running through it: oil, water, or sewage?"

"Man, you need to come down to earth."

"That's what you need to do. While you're under the spell of that incessant beat, the world is moving on, man. Becoming more and more sophisticated. This progress ain't gonna wait for you or me to get hip. Stop waiting and whining, no one will be remunerated for past injustices."

"What you mean, remunerated?"

"See what I mean."

"Aw, man, why you dissin' me?"

"Man, I'm trying to be like you."

"Man, you ain't," he mutters as he sits down.

"THE ONLY WAY TO LEARN JAZZ is by playing, and listening to those who can play. Even though you might not hear any on the radio, you have to seek out the best recordings and go to hear musicians when they come to town. Listening to musicians play live and learning all of the nuances of

selected solos should form the basic vocabulary of your musical style. I'll write out a list for you." The bell rings. School is out, but everyone stays.

"Can y'all play another one for us?" "Let Roy play. Let Roy play." "Check out Roy." "Get him, Roy." Whenever there are exceptional soloists, all of the kids know it and encourage them.

We all fall into a blues. The hunger and enthusiasm these kids play with make me want to go home and practice.

AT THE UNIVERSITY OF NORTH CAROLINA Professor Jim Ketch had his students ready. They played an authentic transcription of Billy Strayhorn's "The Eighth Veil." And they were swinging. I got a chance to conduct the band.

"Always try to understand the function of your part in the music. . . . Make this crescendo with more drama. . . . Sit up and get a good sound out of your horn. . . . Play with more fire, and crisply. Yass! . . . Give me more of my trombones. Make sure to play with more accentuation as you play softer. . . . We need a little more wood out of our bass. Yeah, man, that's it. Unplug your amp, because the band should set its volume to the bass. If you can't hear the bass, you are playing too loud. . . . Put more of yourself into the music. Swing through the whole tune. Swinging is a matter of concentration and constant coordination with style. Swing at all cost. . . . I think that mouthpiece is too shallow, you need to play on a bigger one to produce a more clarion tone. . . . Play this music with confidence. There it is! There it is. Don't let it go."

"What is the meaning of jazz?"

"A swinging dialogue between concerned parties whose philosophy is 'Let's try to work it out.' "

"What is your father doing?"

"You mean right now?"

"You know what I mean."

"He's doing fine, swinging as always. And with a vibe."

"How do you feel about your brother being on Jay Leno?"

"Now I know somebody on TV."

"What did you think about your brother playing with Sting?"

"I didn't think about it."

"Do you feel he sold out?"

"How can someone from our generation sell out? To sell out implies that you have violated a standard that celebrates integrity."

"I like Sting," this one says. Another student wants to know, "Do you play any progressive jazz, like Kenny G.?"

"No, we play real jazz. Kenny G. plays instrumental pop music, which is not to say that it's bad, just not jazz."

"I like Kenny G.'s music," he says. Another asks, "What kind of trumpet is that?"

"It's made by Dave Monette and weighs about seven pounds. It's called the Raja Trumpet. The mouthpiece is built in. Monette says he got the design from his cat, Sheldon."

"Did your daddy make you practice?"

"He's too hip for that. Besides, he was too busy practicing himself. He led by example."

"What do you do when your lips get tired?"

"Stop playing."

"If it's in the middle of a song?"

"Keep playing and take deeper breaths."

"How do you play on chord changes?"

"Listen to the progression and create melodies that fit. Don't think of the chords individually. In most cases you don't play on a succession of chords but a progression. Develop the ability to hear and react to the bass motion. Everything is contingent upon developing your ears."

"What do you think about rap music?"

"Not again."

"I'm serious."

"Nothing."

"I like rap music. You don't think there's room for rap?"

"If it's out there, there's room."

"What do you think about Spike Lee?"

"I don't know anything about movies."

"How can I start listening to real jazz?"

"Buy these CDs. Jelly Roll Morton, "The Pearls." Louis Armstrong, "Hot Five" and "Hot Seven." Count Basie, "The Complete Decca Recordings." John Coltrane, "Crescent." Charlie Parker, "The Complete Dial Recordings." Miles Davis, "Kind of Blue." Thelonious Monk, "It's Monk's Time." Duke Ellington, "Far East Suite." Ornette Coleman, "The Shape of Jazz to Come." Listen to the music, not the quality of sound reproduction. Keep checking these out, and slowly the music will reveal itself to you."

"How do you know what music is about without words?"

"You can put words about anything on top of a backbeat, and the music will still be about the backbeat. Words can't translate music. Music must be experienced on its own terms. Just as words carry meaning, and the organization of words into sentences and paragraphs, so, too, do notes and rhythms and the organization of them into melodies, phrases, and compositions."

I left here feeling very good because of the excellent quality of the band. All praise to Professor Ketch.

"WHAT DO YOU THINK about European jazz?"

"If it's swinging and has some blues in it, I love it."

"No, I mean the free style of improvisation."

"Many musics have improvisation, so it is possible for musicians to improvise without playing jazz. Are they trying to swing?"

"No, but it's not always necessary to swing."

"In jazz it is always necessary to be able to swing consistently and at different tempos. You cannot develop jazz by not playing it, not swinging or playing the blues. Today's jazz criticism celebrates as innovation forms of music that don't address the fundamentals of the music. But no one will create a new style of jazz by evading its inherent difficulties."

"Who determines what jazz is?"

"Those who can best articulate its identity on bandstands."

"So all the avant-garde musicians and critics are wrong and you're right, huh?"

"No, the musicians are right, they know they're not playing jazz. Anthony Braxton, Cecil Taylor, Art Ensemble of Chicago, Steve Coleman, David Sanborn, Miles Davis—when he was still with us—have all said, repeatedly, that they don't play jazz and don't want to. It's the critics who insist that their music is jazz. And since the philosophy that celebrates imitating pop musics or the classical music avant-garde as jazz has become prevalent, how many real jazz musicians, who can swing and play some blues, have been produced? How many true virtuosos of jazz? How many bands that can swing all night long? How many already great jazzmen do you hear sounding like themselves, all night, instead of slipping into retreads of the newest pop hit? What about recordings?"

"So you think jazz is dying?"

"No, this is just a transition. If jazz was dying, nobody would bother reissuing great performances on CDs. Musicians—and advertisers— around the world would not profile on the sophistication implied in its name. If the music was dying, younger musicians would not be interested in learning it. You wouldn't be here today, and neither would I. Jazz music is not dying. Struggling under a weight of misconceptions, but not dying."

"Your definition of jazz is too narrow."

"Who isn't included in it?"

"Lester Bowie, electric Miles Davis, M-Base."

"All those gentlemen have said they don't play jazz. Why disrespect their wishes by insisting that they're wrong?"

"Oh."

"Do you still think my definition is narrow?"

"Yes."

"Why?"

"Everybody says so."

"Oh."

"You said there was no such thing as European jazz."

"I said you can't form a branch of a tree by ignoring the trunk."

"What chance does a European player have to be a great jazz musician?"

"That is up to the musician. When I was growing up, I thought classical music was only for white people. At the age of thirteen I heard a tape of Maurice André, and I wanted to play like him. I didn't search for a school of black musicians who might, by an enormous stretch of the imagination, be said to play like him. I wanted to play like Maurice André. When someone said, 'That's only for white people,' I said, 'I want to play like Maurice André.' When someone said, 'You'll never be accepted in that world,' I said, 'I want to play like Maurice André.' If anyone disrespected Maurice, he had a fight on his hands. Learning to play any music is a matter of practice, insight, desire, and diligence. If you want to swing and play the blues, don't compromise your vision because it seems impossible."

"Why are the best jazz musicians black?"

"As Crouch says, 'They invented it.' People who invent something are always the best at doing it, at least until other folks figure out what it is. America made the best cars for decades, until it forgot the essence of the manufacturing system it had created. Swinging the blues is about culture, not race. If you celebrate less accomplished musicians because you share

a superficial bond, you cheat yourself. Anyway, if you ask most black Americans today who is their favorite jazz musician, they will name some instrumental pop musician. So much for race. The younger musicians of any racial group today swing in spite of their race, not because of it."

"Are you saying white musicians can't play jazz?"

"Jazz includes everyone. That is further proof of its greatness. It accepts and nourishes all who want to participate."

"Why are you so serious?"

"Because, as Mr. Murray says, culture is life-style, and wars are fought over what style of life a society will lead."

"You sound like you don't like pop music, but jazz was pop music in the 1930s, and musicians like Miles Davis always played pop songs."

"If you listen to the 1964 version of Miles playing 'Stella by Starlight,' you barely recognize the melody. He treats the song like a folk theme on which he will perform the art of jazz: elaborate, extend, and refine with blues-based development. His solo leaves the pop song behind; the harmonies are restructured. The band also improvises, and you can hear the spontaneous decisions of group improvisation. When he covers 'Human Nature,' that's a different story. He sticks close to the original arrangement so that maybe he will get a hit. There is little or no interaction with the band. And the song itself is not as rich in improvisational materials as 'Stella by Starlight.' "

"I disagree."

"Have you heard the earlier recording?"

"No."

"Check it out, then come to your own opinion."

"Miles has a right to change."

"I don't challenge that right."

"I like Miles's 'Human Nature.' "

"That's okay. Maybe you'd like 'Stella' even more."

"Don't confuse me with the facts, my mind is made up," he insists. Someone else chimes in, "You sound like a purist."

"Jazz purist is a term created to preserve the integrity of the corrupted. The purist is scorned as closed-minded and regressive, so that those who lack artistic integrity can get rich and feel persecuted at the same time. Purists have no money, no power, no avenues to disseminate their views, and no influence, yet they are constantly attacked by those who do."

"Why do you play Dixieland?"

"We don't play Dixieland. We play New Orleans music. This music puts us in closer contact with the spirit and meaning of jazz. New Orleans music uses all the idiomatic devices of jazz: riffs, breaks, call and response, vamps, solos, grooves, polyphonic improvisation, and chorus format. It remains the most modern extension of the Western music tradition because you can hear whole groups negotiate with each other, making intelligent and unintelligent decisions while grooving.

"Group improvisation means that everyone takes chances, dancing rhythms against the hardwood floor of the form, together attempting to step elegantly through the obstacles of bad musical judgment. One must be forgiving and resilient, have good ears and quick reflexes. That suits the modern world; find an interesting idea, but be ready to change if fresh evidence disproves it or elevates it.

"You have to play this music with soul, and that's fun. It's fun to listen to another person stretching out and to go right on out on the limb yourself. Or to push them out. Way out on a limb with music is a hip place to be. And people like this music because it's joyous. The groove is happy and Herlin knows how to play it. Swing is a collective decision. That is why we play New Orleans music."

"What do you like better, jazz or classical music?"

"Jazz."

"Because jazz has more feeling?"

"No. Classical music conveys a wide range of deeply felt experiences. But jazz is more modern and ancient. Jazz is harmony through conflict, like a good, hot discussion."

"You talk about technique, but not about feeling."

"You know how you feel. To express your feelings, just don't be shy. Sometimes the discussion of feeling is used to cloak laziness. As Paul Hindemith said, 'The impulse or feeling of an artist must be very small if it is manifest in such little knowledge.' But, of course, I know that doesn't apply to you."

"Young musicians today have a lot of technique, but they haven't picked up the feeling of jazz in the streets or in the clubs like the older ones, isn't that so?"

"Not at all. If anything, the older musicians were much more technical. Clifford Brown, Clark Terry, Freddie Webster, Booker Little, Lee Morgan had highly developed technique. Not to mention Dizzy or Pops. Miles and Monk went to Juilliard. Jimmy Blanton took lessons from symphony bassists all around the world. Wayne Shorter went to New York University. Coleman Hawkins studied the cello. Jazz musicians have always respected scholarship.

"The greatest lesson was the chance to take a master class by hearing a practicing virtuoso on the bandstand. Louis Armstrong sat at the feet of Joe Oliver, Charlie Parker at the feet of Lester Young, Buster Smith, and Chu Berry. Johnny Hodges learned from Sidney Bechet. Sweets Edison, Rex Stewart, Ray Nance, Cootie Williams, and Bunny Berrigan learned from Louis Armstrong, and so on.

"The lives of young musicians are not less confused or painful or emotional than those of older musicians. It is just that the means of expressing their lives has been corrupted by cultural celebration of the insignificant. There have always been many types of jazzmen from the hell-raisers like Sidney Bechet and Fats Waller to the pious like Lawrence Brown, the humorous like Dizzy Gillespie, the intellectual like Coleman Hawkins, the drug addicted like Charlie Parker, and the downright nice like Clifford Brown.

"Today's musicians are equally diverse. The problem is not their technique or emotion, but the impoverished cultural soil in which they must grow. They are trying hard, but get very little help. Play the blues and swing, if you want to play jazz. Please don't go looking to pay dues and think it will make your playing soulful. Soul is honest expression, with warmth. Soul is a spiritual proposition. Soul means you make other people feel good."

"Play something for us."

"With pleasure."

The blues has a twelve-bar form.

To improvise means attempting to improve and working with whatever is available.

Swing is a matter of ongoing coordination and participation.

The ultimate achievement in jazz soloing in the expression of a distinctive personality.

The ultimate achievement in jazz music is the interplay of distinctive personalities through some type of musical form. The group establishes its identity with this interplay while swinging.

Jazz is musical interplay on blues-based melodies, harmonies, rhythms, and textures in the motion of an improvised groove. A groove is the successful coordination of differing parts—like a clock. That's a vamp.

"Why do you all wear suits? Is that some kind of statement?"
"It looks good. That's the only reason." That's a tag.

THE SOUND OF HUMAN FEELING has a power and intensity of its own. The power in jazz comes from the passionate intelligence of a group of musicians playing together. Musical freedom of speech. This has a timeless quality. The technology of the human soul does not change like an automobile or computer. That's why loud, overamplified sound defeats the main purpose of jazz, to invite the audience into a group's emotion, not to impose it on them. Volume gives the illusion of a power you have not earned and cannot control. That's a coda.

10. CRESCENDOS AND

For Crouch

I might have heard,
but I didn't listen.

THEY ARE OLD OAK TREE OF MEN. Strong, proud, with far-reaching roots deeply embedded, sucking nourishment from the original stream, their branches stretching out boldly against the sky to proclaim the majesty of the blues. You could walk right past a big ol' tree and never look, let alone see. It's always been there, silent, listening, still but ever changing, waiting to tell you what you need to know, emitting ageless information on a frequency detected by only the most sensitive ears.

Yet all you have to do is ask. A humble request puts you on the wavelength to untold libraries of riches. Knowledge pours out on that frequency, as thickly and quickly as a can of paint toppled from a sky-high ladder, to fill the empty recesses of your spotted soul. Quickly and thickly, as if years of neglect will be washed away in an awkward moment by the attention of one who wants to understand. Awkward only because you are not ready for the too-quick rush of such valued information.

The eager sharing of this wisdom implies a deep and profound loneliness. Ask earnestly, and the telling of ancient secrets becomes commonplace. They are the elders, unimpressed but hopeful. They have seen important things come and go. They'll tell you, "Those who play for applause, that's all they get." They'll tell you, "Don't ask why is it, but what is it?" Yes, what. They are what was. But they still are, like warriors forced

DIMINUENDOS

to fight past their prime (because of weakness in the youth), who become one with their cause, proclaiming the majesty of the blues, the jazz blues. Not by playing or telling but by being big ol' oak tree of men.

Old-style Negroes. Hat-wearing, shoe-shined, vine-pressed, thin-mustached, hair-swept, sweet-cologne-smelling, thin-razor-shaved, willfully sophisticated Americans of all persuasions for all occasions—Negroes. Art Blakey said it: "No America, no jazz."

What do you do when something that was, still is? Like your ex-woman that you still love? These men let you know that "what is" is inescapable. They are masters of the present tense. Old, seasoned warriors in the unwinnable battle with Father Time, they have swung, still swing. They accept weakness in the young but do not excuse it. They stride proudly through the social decay of the late twentieth century, with its fake air of informality put on to cloak a lack of grace and style, and of sophistication. They are direct descendants of the original jazzmen, here to proclaim the majesty of the blues, the jazz blues.

Tales of old are exchanged not in words but in gestures. Soul gestures. Do not misconstrue the sadness in their eyes as a sign of defeat. It is the mark of a profound loneliness, the heroic loneliness of those who sustain an intense relationship with a reality so harsh as to burn the eyes of the unprepared who chance to look upon it. Look closer and you will see a timeless joy in these oak tree of men. Through music, they have touched divine intelligence, and that is their identity. Blakey let you know, "From the Creator to the artist to you."

They bear no titles or fancy positions, they are called by first name or nickname or last name alone: Dizzy, C. T., Art, Klook, Papa Jo, Pops, Lil' Jazz, Sweets, Frog, Trane, Pres, Jackie, Elvin, Bean, Count, Duke, Monk, Mingus, Tatum. These names identify not only persons but sounds, inimitable, personal sounds that communicate ancient, modern, and most obvious fundamentals through the abstract language of jazz music, through the concrete language of the blues.

Tales so old as to be new are exchanged not in words but in gestures, soul gestures. Words are too imprecise to convey how their world feels. Soul gestures are habit—beyond thought (and that is where they preside).

Not the obvious posturing of the would-be hip like the "Hey, baby" of copy-cat slang or the overbite of profanity, but the quiet and unseen grace of the prayer before a meal, the careful shaving of a reed, or the days and nights of practice, study, and reflection.

Have you ever heard of a hipster practicing? Sweets Edison will tell you, "I *learned* how to play." Art Blakey would tell you, "Stay until you digest the information. Digested information is knowledge. Knowledge is power." Not the power to subjugate or purchase, but the power to enlighten. He would growl, "You never see an armored car following a hearse."

Yes, a true hipster. Not the fraudulent, would-be hip hitmen of media and commerce but real-life, old-style oak tree of men whose hipness flows from unsurrendering battle with the realities of American life. What is the position of the genius whose observations stand as accurate testimonies on the power of the American spirit in the twentieth century, who is also a . . . yes, a nigger? Is that what we say? We Americans? Yes. But not all together, though. In our separate quarters, and with feeling.

Charlie Parker was a genius, was a junkie. He died young. But these are old oak tree of men, unimpressed, accepting of tragedy, unfazed warriors, still on the battlefield swinging in style.

Squares and would-be hipsters write and talk of Bunk, Lee, Spanky, or Philly Joe as if the mere mention of a nickname and the retailing of a stale anecdote give them entrée into this plantation walk of oak trees. They do not. The would-be hip identify themselves as squares by the partial telling of the tale. They refuse to understand that the manifestation of a thing is not the thing itself. They preen themselves in the shade of these great oaks, but are deaf to ancient wisdoms freely available to any who ask humbly and truly want to know. The arrogance of the would-be hip cloaks the fear that they will be told what they already know or suspect.

"To hate a thing that you love, destroys. Not just the object of your ardent affection and loathing, but you. Yourself tied in a mysterious bond with what you will destroy. So kill it if you must, but realize that as it dies, so, too, do you, or a vital portion of yourself." How does Manhattan feel about Harlem now? Is it the same Harlem of the jungle fantasies?

The elders will tell you, "Black and white, not brown, that's the down-fall of America." Danny Barker will tell you, "Watch yourself. You may choose this battlefield, but many a good man has fallen here, white and black." Mr. Murray will tell you, "Americans are mulattoes. All Americans." What is a pure American anyway? you ask.

What is a pure anything that is always in the process of becoming itself? The elders will tell you, "It is the integrity of that process. The will to interact with style." What is a pure American Negro? "The man with one drop of Negro blood."

"Why, that's a white man," you say. No, that is the purest form of the American Negro, according to time-honored Jim Crow definition. You see, American Negrohood is a matter not of race but of culture. That's why its name changes every five years.

"That's not today. You're talking about the past. We are now New Africans," the would-be hip say. Yes, black and white, that's the downfall of America, not brown. Doc Cheatham will tell you he doesn't know or care what color people are. He can remember carrying King Oliver's horn down the streets of Azo's Chicago. He comes to swing and play with a big, clarion sound. Art Blakey let you know: "No America, no jazz."

What is pure jazz? The elders will tell you, "The integrity of the process of individuals willfully sophisticating the blues together."

"That could be anything," the would-be hip say. Yes, it could be anything, if that's what you want to believe. A thing can be many ways, but it can also not be itself. Like the one drop of Negro blood. Black and white, this is the spiritual downfall of America. Jefferson said it in so many words.

Old oak tree of men, they are seasoned warriors whose hipness flows from unsurrendering battle with the realities of American life. Unafraid, unimpressed. They proudly wear the battle scars inflicted by a society that resentfully projects negative intentions onto them as punishment for their willful sophistication. For being Americans, free and using that freedom to set others free. Audacious, not giving a damn, these oaks atomize hate and jealousy by proclaiming the majesty of the blues. They have one thing to tell those who would also be battle-tested warriors, "If a thing is not itself, does not want to be itself, your job is to raise its consciousness to self-acceptance."

Blacks love their blackness, whites love their whiteness, but that is the false rallying cry of the unhip and the would-be hip, the rabble-rousers and the unrighteous in search of a constituency. That is the unnourishing past, the big lie in the human march toward the divine.

There will be no revenge. Americans are mulattoes. Whether we hate or are indifferent to each other, that is our reality. It is the reality of jazz music born in the too-hot, smoked pot of gumbo that is New Orleans, Louisiana, where creoles, dark-skinned Negroes, white folks, Indians, and others were cooked in a roux called the blues.

Jelly Roll Morton said a Negro was dumber than two dead police dogs in somebody's backyard. Forced to integrate by circumstance, seething with hate, victimized by prejudice, rife with ignorance, fearful, strained and steamed by the disdainful violation of the Declaration of Independence, the Bill of Rights, and the Constitution of the United States of

America, these people, these Americans, these niggers willed an art into existence to objectify the most precious aspirations of democratic thought, and to validate those same conceptions so compromised in their daily lives as to seem absurd. Seem but not be. This they knew: all men and women are created equal and endowed with the right, hell, the responsibility, to swing.

The original jazzmen depended on this. Now, voting is too great a request. But these people wanted to understand and enjoy the liberties and responsibilities of citizenship, because a thing is always more precious and desirable when you don't have it. Like water or food or romance, or yes, freedom, lest we forget.

This is the majesty of the blues. The excluded include themselves through a skillful display of insight into the most fundamental of American realities, travelling like Cinderella from the kitchen to the castle, by way of soul. Soul gestures.

This is jazz music, created not by slavery but by its abolition and the oh-so-human will to freedom. That is the sound of a band swinging.

What do you do when the clearest objectification of who you are

comes from what you hate? What do you do? Not recognize it? What do you do when you are inseparable from what you hate?

Willful participation with style and in the groove. That is the process—swinging.

Clark Terry will tell you, "Work on this plunger till you can make a trumpet talk." Art Farmer will tell you, "Listen and pick the pretty notes. Shut up and listen." Jackie McLean will tell you, "If something ain't cool with the music, you

have to say it ain't cool. That's the only way it will get better." Marcus Belgrave will tell you, "You have to be happy about living to swing." Jimmie Heath will tell you, "Pick one note and learn how it sounds in all of the rest of the keys. Then pick another and another until you run out." He'll also say, "This is how Pres did it." One warrior loves to recount the exploits of another. They form a fraternity; each reinforces some part of the other, in life and death. They are few in number, but they love being old oak tree of men. Deep rooted, with branches swinging, with or without the wind.

Barry Harris will tell you, "D-flat to C to E-9 to F-7 and -13 to B-flat major. Yes, and now the bridge." He will give you the correct melodies to tunes that you have incorrectly played and make sure you've got it. The elders are unimpressed but hopeful. Elvin Jones will tell you, "I love you." He will tell you, "Don't you ever bullshit. Stop whining and play. Play." You will ask him, "How am I doing?" He will tell you, "See me in twenty years and I'll let you know."

Seasoned warriors, their hipness flows from unsurrendering battle with the realities of American life. Modern life, late in the twentieth. Those who have not surrendered take on the special glow of warriors forced to fight past their time (because of weakness in the youth), who become one with their cause, proclaiming proudly the majesty of the blues. Many have surrendered, attempting after defeat was assured to gain a measure of comfort before the final bar. Convinced the too-long battle was not worth the trouble.

Have you ever fought for those who are deaf and blind to their own reality? Ask these old-style, Southern-hat-wearing, thick-belted, proper-speaking, no-shit-taking, romance-loving, don't mind dying Negroes how it feels to walk unrecognized and disrespected through any and every Afro-American neighborhood. Ask them how the decay of what they have fought for so valiantly smells and feels, ask them, what about America? Their answer will be the same: "We accept tragedy without whining. Problems are opportunities. We are here to proclaim the majesty of the blues."

Better yet, ask one who has surrendered. He can better describe the feeling of neglect, having succumbed to it. He is still a warrior, albeit a fallen one. Now more celebrated in defeat. Ask, if you want to know the

pitiful truth of surrender after a too-long struggle with forces that have always been unbeatable—forces of prejudice, of ignorance, of apathy, greed, the inhumane. But you probably can't find the words. How do you talk to an old fallen warrior who has surrendered senselessly, soon after defeat was assured, surrendered before the good fighting begins, the fight for the life of a thing? Now he tours the world in a cage to represent the grandeur of those who have defeated him, an old Hannibal in the hands of the Romans. Trapped in his own fame, and on display Miles away from his capitulation. Now the tales of his victories are exaggerated because they no longer honor himself, but his captors, who will graciously define him and his generations. That is the way of war.

But that undeniable truth of America first objectified in sound a hundred years ago in New Orleans, Louisiana, will summon warriors regard-

less of circumstance. Too many willful participants have engaged in the lifelong struggle to raise to consciousness an unwilling nation. So even as the fallen proclaim, "I had to change with the times," or "So what?" the old oaks stand tall and proud. Slightly bent but not yielding, they proclaim the majesty of the blues. And this act of defiance, no, affirmation, produces somewhere in the no-matter-how-weak young a desire to take to the field of battle armed only with a sound and a determination to swing, no matter how senseless.

Then the sharing of ancient wisdoms becomes commonplace. So common as to belie a deep and profound loneliness, and imply a plea for acceptance and understanding. These are the elders, unimpressed but hopeful. They have seen important things come and go. Accepting of tragedy, unfazed warriors still on the battlefield, they swing the blues through the social decay of the late twentieth century, with its fake air of informality put on to cloak the lack of grace and style and sophistication and soul, yes, of soul. They are masters of the present tense, unyielding, unafraid, invulnerable. Strong, proud, with far-reaching roots deeply embedded. Do not misconstrue the sadness in their eyes as the sign of defeat. It marks the heroic loneliness of those who sustain an intense relationship with a reality so harsh as to burn the eyes of the unprepared who would dare look upon it.

What do you do when something that was, still is? Not recognize it? They are the illuminati, a thankless job. If you enter a room of people shrouded in darkness and turn on a light, they will only cover their eyes and curse—not just you, the light itself.

Look close and you will see a timeless joy in these ol' oak tree of men. They have touched divine intelligence through music, and that is their identity. They were born to proclaim the majesty of the blues, and it is how they will go down, swinging. What a glorious way to go. And if you pay close enough attention, they might just let you swing with 'em.

MY FATHER always used to say, "If you're gonna get beat up, you might as well fight."

11. WOODSHEDDING

racticing is the first sign of
morality in a musician.

AS A BOY I loved the way my daddy and all of the jazz musicians spoke. The lingo was an important part of their hipness. One of their favorite and inescapable words was "shed," which rhymes with "head."

"Yeah, man, I been shedding, hard." "Let's shed on this." "Man, you need to go shed."

Somewhere around eleven years old, I realized that shedding meant getting in the woodshed, practicing. By the time I was sixteen, I understood what the shed was about—hard, concentrated work.

At first, shedding is truly painful, 'cause you can't play and you have to concentrate on that fact. You're always working on something undesirable in your musical personality. You're by yourself, in a corner, listening for imperfections and trying to clarify them. And you know you're going to be practicing for a long time. You don't see immediate progress. You can't go out and have fun when you want to. You can't just skip shedding for weeks at a time. It's like being on a diet. You keep going slowly, slowly up the hill.

When Branford and I auditioned for our high school band, the band instructor, George Marks, was excited about Ellis's sons coming to the band. (My father was an underground hero on the local scene.) After I played my audition it was so pitiful he said, "Are you sure you're Ellis's son?"

His comment didn't affect me that much, because I was more interested in basketball than music. But somewhere along the line I started listening to John Coltrane and decided to try becoming a musician. It was time to get into the woodshed. Deep in the shed.

I didn't miss a day of practice for seven years. And after that, still not too many. I wrote out a schedule for practicing all the fundamental aspects of technique: tonguing, tone, slurring, velocity, and so on. My practice sessions punctuated the day, going from the most fundamental techniques to the most complex.

First, breathing exercises. Then long tones that incorporate breathing. Flexibility drills, which include long tones and breathing. Tonguing, which includes long tones, breathing, and flexibility. Then the characteristic and lyrical studies that allow you to work on all of these things. Finally I did the solos, like the Haydn or the Brandenburg, or a Clifford Brown solo, and tried to focus on all of the techniques I had worked on through the day. After that I would have a gig or a rehearsal. Every day, at least three hours a day, and often four or five. And I discovered I still had a lot of time to pursue interesting avenues of social intercourse.

The time spent on a particular technique was based on my ability to execute it. Things I could correctly play quickly, I wouldn't practice that much. Those I couldn't do at all, much longer. Solving technical problems is an intellectual proposition as much as it is physical. You have to figure out how to practice problems away.

Teaching is important. On Saturdays I took lessons from John Longo, Norman Smith, or George Jansen. They were great teachers. I learned all of the fundamentals of playing from them, and also every now and then from Bill Fielder (he taught at Mississippi Valley State and showed me how to play the piccolo trumpet). Most important, they taught me that you must solve the most difficult problems yourself. To develop as a musician, you have to not mind doing the work. As Mr. Murray always says, "Everybody wants to be the hero, but they don't want to slay the dragon." Shedding is preparation to face the dragon. You still might not make it out alive, but at least you have a chance.

WRITING IS THE SAME AS PRACTICING. Concentration and diligence are required. You hear a sound, then pursue it in the most direct fashion. When it's on the page, you play with it just like you played with all sorts of inanimate objects as a child. You play with the notes, rhythms, chords, and textures, even the personalities of the musicians.

"Try this for me. Cone, play C; Wes, play B-natural; and Todd, play that E-flat above it. What you think about that?"

"I played a D-natural instead of an E-flat."

"Try the E-flat."

"The D sounds better, I think."

"Yeah, let's keep the D. Thanks."

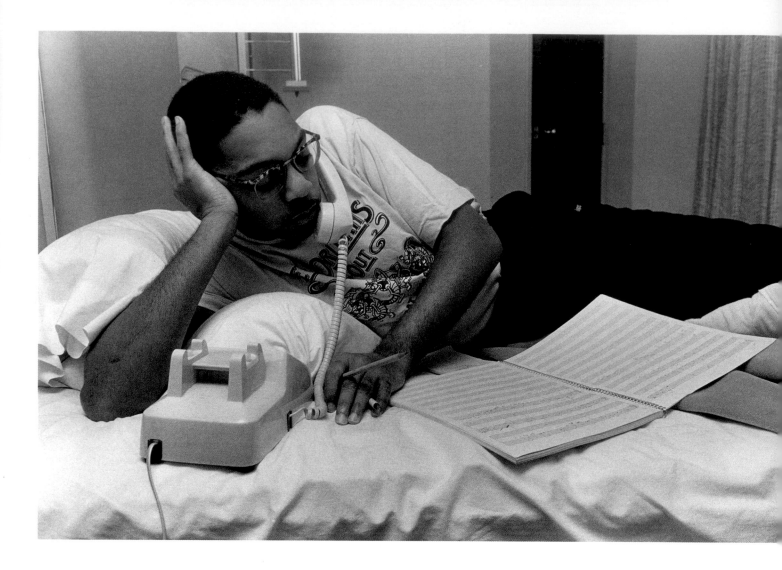

WORDS THAT SWEET demanded a soundtrack.

MUSIC COMES TO YOU AT strange times but you have to be ready to catch it, because if you don't, she may be gone for good. Until the next time.

Ronnie Carbo copies our music. He is from New Orleans, and he loves to play the bass and dance to second-line music. You can see how hard he concentrates. I give him scores that look like a Rorschach test. He makes them look pristine.

WE WILL SHED ANYWHERE.

"Damn, man. That's a low A-flat. That's impossible to play this fast."

"Man, what's your name?"

"Say, man, what does this mean?"

"What?"

"It just says 'Veal.' "

"That means just be Veal in that spot."

"Well, what do you want?"

"Whatever you hearin'."

"Say, Skayne, you have to change this melody. It's kind of corny."

"What do you mean?"

"Listen to it. You can't have Warm Daddy wasting all his good hot soulful sound on nothing like that."

"Play what you want, man. Play what you want."

"Check these notes."

"Can we get something to drink?"

"You want plunger here?"

"Let me hear it. Hmm. What do you think?"

"Plunger."

"Okay."

"I think we should go to the swing right here. Then back to the groove."

"Let's hear it. . . . That's cool."

"Okay, I see what this is."

"Let's go to measure 136."

"What time is it?" "Man, let's go get some of those hamburgers from around the corner." "This is some hard music, man, you must be crazy."

WHENEVER I PLAY with Branford, I think of us growing up in Kenner, Louisiana, playing the clarinet and the trumpet. We played duets out of the Arban *Complete Method for Trumpet,* "Air by Mozart," "Air by Handel." We didn't have any idea who Mozart and Handel were, we couldn't even pronounce their names, we'd say *Mose*-art, Han-*dell*.

In high school we played together in a funk band, the Creators. We played many, many dances, weddings, proms, battles of the bands, and talent shows, and had a thoroughly good time socially. We loved playing together. We could play horn parts real, real tight, and with a vibe.

But even more than playing together, we grew up together a certain way. Our personalities developed to fit each other. I was hot and fiery, ready to curse somebody out and tell him to kiss my ass. Book was cool and diplomatic: "Man, if you just shut your mouth, we'll be cool."

Branford could eat, too. Yes, indeed, any and everything. Boy, you have a pot roast, he'll eat the whole thing. You'll come in, and the roast'll be gone. Long gone.

We slept in the same room until Branford went off to college. That was the loneliest year of my life. I was so used to going to bed, talking to Branford, "Say, Book, you know what, man?" I was always the last one to sleep. He had to have music on or he couldn't sleep, and I could never sleep until it was off. So I waited for him to sleep, every night. I didn't like sleeping anyway, still don't. Always feel like I'm missing something.

We played a lot of gigs, so we were used to getting home at one or two o'clock in the morning. Our mama would leave us something to eat, and we would come in all late, ready to talk about the gig.

"How was the gig?"

"Good, Mama, good."

"Good, I left something on the stove for y'all. Just heat it up."

Then we'd go to making all kinds of noise.

"Boy, y'all stop makin' all of that noise before you wake those children up. Close that door. What time is it? Coming in all hours of the night."

Sometimes it'd be hard. You'd get home at 1:00, 1:30, and have to get up at 6:30 to start shedding. That'd be a rough transition. Yeah, me and Book had us plenty of good times. On and off of bandstands.

RECORDING PUTS YOU ON EDGE, you're a little nervous because you know it's being documented. When I'm recording, sometimes I curse cats out and am a real pain in the butt. I used to apologize to the cats before we went into the studio. "Man, please forgive me. You know we got to get a lot done in a short amount of time. If I get on my vibe, please don't be mad, you know I love y'all."

In Delfeayo's recording session I got into the crouch I used to play in. I had stopped playing like that, but I reverted to it a little taste, because Delfeayo likes it. Branford likes it, too: "Go ahead, get in your crouch, man, get in your crouch." Sometimes you get so tangled up in the music, you have to apply a little body English.

GENERALLY AT SOUND CHECKS WE drive Rob crazy. He wants the sound check to be orderly, and we always act real nonchalant. We switch instruments, come in late, fool around. Veal takes fifteen minutes to take the bass out. Rob calls it "my sound check. I'm trying to conduct my sound check, and you all are bullshitting. Why is that happening?" We respond by being silent for a moment, then slowly disintegrating into cacophony and pandemonium. I played tuba in one sound check.

The sound check could be over in five minutes, if we didn't mess around. But that may be impossible. At the sound check you get a feeling for the venue. You are less nervous and the concert flows more smoothly if you are familiar with the surroundings. I'll also take advantage of having the band together to rehearse something. Rob hates that, so he and I always have a heated exchange.

"Let me hear Wes."

"Man, can't you see I'm trying to rehearse?"

"This is my sound check, man. How do you want to sound tonight? Call a real rehearsal."

Rob is serious as a heart attack. He loves to work. You have to be serious to be great at something. That's why rehearsing is important. Too much disrespecting of rehearsing people's music goes on out here. If you don't want to play some music, stay home. We know how important it is to rehearse.

That's the thing I never liked about playing with orchestras. At four o'clock sharp, everyone stops in the middle of a phrase, picks up his or her instrument, and walks off the stage—union rules. Not the Cleveland Symphony Orchestra. They stay and rehearse, they want to sound great. All the time. Yes.

12. TWELFTH BAR

If you are fortunate enough to find an iron, you commence pressing your brand-new white suit. Then, just as you are about to step into it and admire the profile of your creased trousers, you notice that the iron has a big brown stain on it. And now so does your suit.

"YES, SIR, we'll have the ironing board sent up right away." One hour later you are left to improvise an ironing board. You iron your black pants, and then you notice . . . the lint from the towels is all over your pants. And you have to look at that ugly-ass carpet.

YOU ARE REALLY SAYING, "It is 7:40 P.M. My room service has not arrived. I am starving. Late for the gig. And the button on my right sleeve just fell off." But you smile because then you think, "I have a gig. Tonight." That feels good. Damned good.

YOU'VE BEEN ON THE ROAD for three weeks. Your hair is uncut, unmanageable, and uneven. So you brush it and then pat it down in 2/4 time. Ultimately to no avail.

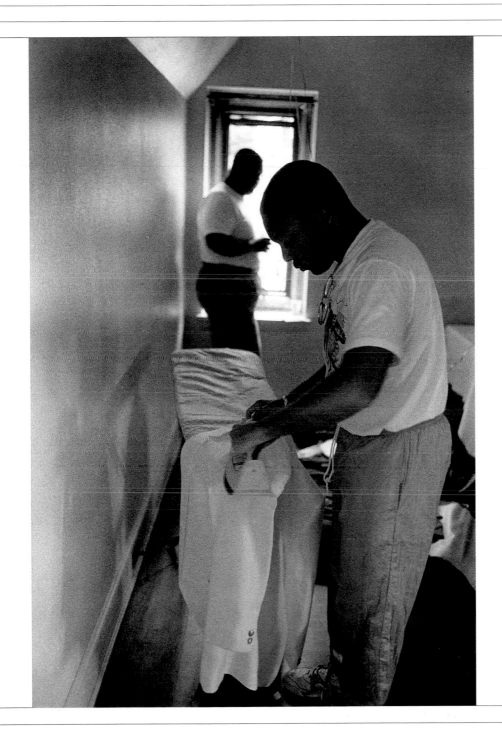

YOU PULL YOUR HORN OUT. Blow a few self-inflicted notes. Adjust your reeds, slides, and ties. And prepare to face the blues on high ground.

"D to G to E-flat to A-flat to B-natural to E-natural to . . ."

    "Are you sure?"

    "Man, what is my name?"

YOU PLAY SOFTLY, trying to think of some preliminary order for tonight's engagement. You may have the opportunity to flirt with some unsuspecting passerby, playing one of the favorite melodies of the region. And then again, perhaps not.